Castellini on Computers

The book that should have come with your computer!

Castellini on Computers

The book that should have come with your computer!

Rick Castellini, MCP

Brivin Press

Manufactured in the United States of America

Library of Congress Control Number: 00-136113
ISBN: 0-9705409-0-6
Illustrations: Brianna L. Castellini
Cover Design: Pearl & Associates
Editing: Tabby House

Brivin Press
2182 I Road
Grand Junction, CO 81505
970-257-0825, fax 253-679-0596
publisher@yourpcpartner.com
www.yourpcpartner.com

To Beth, Brianna, Vinny

Special thanks to Bob Craft and
Dr. Michael Horwitz

Contents

Foreword

I met Rick Castellini several years ago when my wife discovered and hired him to teach her and our young children to use a computer.

At the time, I knew nothing about computers, not even how to turn one on. Within a few weeks, our children developed an intrepid attitude toward computing and surprising skill on our desktop.

I was impressed. Was it because our children were brilliant, or because Rick had some special gift?

Either way, I felt inspired to take the plunge and purchase a laptop. Rick was there to help decide on the right machine for me. When it arrived, he set it up and launched me on my journey to geekdom.

Within days, I was downloading all sorts of seemingly vital software off the Internet. I learned about email, and began pestering friends, and even remote acquaintances, with salvos of bad email jokes. Within weeks, my hard drive was filled to the brim and crashed.

Some people think they are accident-prone. In those early days, I felt crash-prone. But Rick kept coming over, and teaching me valuable lessons and skills. He absolutely ran circles around the software techs I would call through the 800 numbers on my warranties.

There were times that I felt like a bumbling idiot. But Rick treated me with patience and respect.

The answers were made to appear simple. And the learning was easy, always a pleasure. Soon I was confident, highly productive, self-sufficient, and quite knowledgeable. Now, nearly four years later, I still find myself comforted by the fact that I have access Rick to answer my technology questions.

In my profession as a physician, I work with many elderly people who have health problems. Many of these folks are frightened of computers, or believe they are too old to get started. And yet the computer can lead to very valuable sources of information, communication and record keeping.

There are many times when I want a particular patient to have access to the net, so he or she can communicate directly with me, or have access to certain sources of medical information. Consequently, over the past three years, I have referred many computer users to Rick, for assistance in getting set up with and learning to become proficient on a computer. In every instance I get the same feedback: Rick is a great person, extremely helpful and easy to understand.

As I read through this book, I was surprised and delighted again and again to learn new and valuable tools.

This is not the sort of text that needs to be updated every six months. Rather, it gives essential tips and skills. I thought I already knew the basics and essentials, yet there are so many ways to be more productive, facile, and competent.

I challenge you to peruse this book for ten minutes and not come up with something new and useful.

Michael Horwitz, M.D.

Director, Department of Integrative Medicine
Saint Mary's Hospital
Grand Junction, Colorado

Former director, Department of Addiction Medicine
Cedars Sinai Medical Center
Los Angeles, California

A word from the author

Thank you for purchasing this book and allowing me to help you learn how to better use your computer. I have made every effort to write the most practical book you can read on the subject.

You can use the book as a reference and learning manual without reading it cover-to-cover. However, if you decide to read it from start-to-finish, you will follow a logical path to develop comfort and expertise with your computer.

As you read along, you will find many "recipes" to accomplish the most common computer tasks. To maximize your efficiency, the book is organized so you can easily identify your specific software, and quickly learn the skills without wading through irrelevant information.

If you follow the recipes outlined, you will learn the tasks that it describes quickly and painlessly. After all, computers are supposed to facilitate the accomplishment of tasks—efficiently and without stress.

This type of straightforward instruction works. I use it every day in my consulting business to help my clients have great success in becoming happy, proficient computer users.

The most important tip

In its most basic essence, a computer is no different than a car. Your car sits in the garage or on the street until ***you*** turn the key ignition and push down on the accelerator. Likewise, a computer just sits on your desk and does nothing until ***you*** turn it on and give it instructions.

Computer users, particularly new users, feel intimidated by that big beige box sitting on the floor or desk. I am convinced that ***anyone***, with the right frame of mind, can easily learn to use a computer successfully. Reading and using this book will help you attain the proper frame of mind.

Just like a car, ***you*** have complete control over the computer. It does **not** control you. Just like a car, if you get lost or confused with your computer, pause and ask for directions (you've taken the first step by purchasing this book) or drive around and experiment until you get it right.

Bottom line, always remember that you can reach over and shut the blasted machine off. ***You are in the driver's seat***, and help is readily available.

The second most important tip

Computers offer the uncanny ability to accomplish the same task in numerous different ways. If you ask five of your friends how to accomplish a computer task, you may receive five different answers.

There is **no wrong way** to accomplish a computer task.

Keep that small phrase in mind as you use your computer. If you are comfortable tackling a computer task in a certain manner, then don't worry if your neighbor or colleague does something different.

The method you are comfortable with is the correct method.

Demystifying Windows

Microsoft Windows is the most popular software package in the computer world today. Over ninety percent of all computers worldwide use some form of Microsoft Windows. Yet, to many computer users, Microsoft Windows remains as mysterious as the Seven Wonders of the World.

In this section, you will learn all the basics you need to know about Microsoft Windows to become a more productive, confident computer user.

The techniques discussed throughout this section apply to:

- ➲ Windows 95
- ➲ Windows 98
- ➲ Windows 98 SE
- ➲ Windows Me
- ➲ and to a lesser degree to Windows NT and 2000

Your mouse is your friend

Windows makes extensive use of your mouse. Most tasks you perform with your computer will be easier and quicker if you understand how to properly use the mouse. So, even if you are afraid of the small furry variety, you need to be best of friends with your computer mouse!

- POINTER — The shape of the mouse icon that moves around on your screen. Note that most of the time your **pointer** will be an arrow, but it will change during different operations. (Example: while a program is working on a task, the pointer will change to an hourglass OR in an area where text can be entered, it looks like a capital I.)

- CLICK — Push the LEFT button only ONCE while holding the pointer over the target object.

- DOUBLE CLICK — Push the LEFT button TWICE QUICKLY while holding the pointer over the target object.

RIGHT CLICK	Push the RIGHT button only ONCE while holding the pointer over the target object. Windows 95/98 and programs developed for Win95/98 make extensive use of the RIGHT mouse button to call shortcut menus for a particular object; thereby providing easy access to some commands and properties.
DRAG AND DROP	Click and HOLD your LEFT mouse button on the target object and move (drag) the object where you want it and then release the button (drop).
SELECT	Click on an object or drag across text to highlight it.

Click and double-click?

One of the most common questions I am asked week-to-week in my consulting business is, "When do I double-click and when do I single-click my mouse?"

The only place a double-click is *necessary*, with Windows, is on the desktop when starting a program. (And yes, there are even ways around this.)

My advice: click once and only double-click when the single-click does not work.

Why won't my double-click work?

When you receive a computer from the factory or store, your mouse has some preset properties that do not always work for every individual. For a beginner, double-clicking can be not only a frustrating task, but also, in some cases, an impossible one.

Here's how to get that double-click working:

1. Click on START.
2. Click on CONTROL PANEL.
3. Click one time on the MOUSE icon.
4. Push ENTER on your keyboard.
5. Click on the BASICS or MOVEMENT (depending on which mouse you have) tab at the top of the screen and look for the double-click setting.
6. Click with your mouse on this setting and move the bar to the slower end of the scale (this will slow down the speed required in order to effectively double-click) OR double-click *slowly* on the icon if your control looks similar to the following picture.

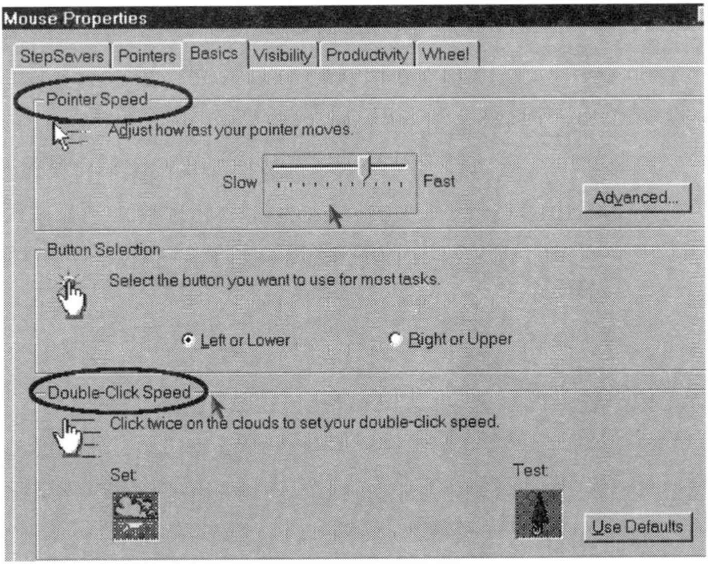

7. Click on APPLY.
8. Click on OK.

Now try double-clicking again (make sure the you're not moving the mouse at the same time) and you should be successful. If not, repeat the procedure above and slow the mouse double-click speed down further.

Tip within a tip:
Instead of double-clicking, try clicking one time on an icon and then press ENTER on your keyboard.

Tip within a tip within a tip:
Some users may find working with a trackball is easier than working with a mouse. Trackballs look like upside down

mice and you move the ball that sits on top instead of the whole mouse.

Another tip within a tip:
Play the included Solitaire game in Windows. Windows includes Solitaire to help users become more adept with the mouse.

Computer lingo

You will learn further details about each of these items as you read this book.

Windows 95/98 The operating environment in which all of your programs are able to run

This is known as the **Windows Desktop**. It is what your screen looks like when you first turn your computer on and can be completely customized to look the way you want it to.

Start button The button that is used to access all of your programs and options within Windows 95/98.

Taskbar

Usually found at the bottom of your desktop, it indicates which programs are currently open.

Icon

Small graphic that represents a computer file or program. Each has a unique set of properties that control it.

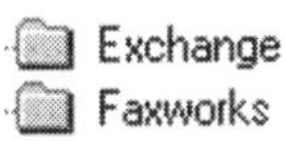

Folders

A folder is simply an area in your computer that contains information (files) for a program or information you created. Each program will have its own folder or folders.

Megabyte A method of measuring how much space a particular file or folder occupies on your computer. Internal computer storage disks (hard drives) are measured in gigabytes. (When you fill up your car with gas, it is measured in gallons. With a computer, the megabyte is the measuring tool.)

1 megabyte=1000 kilobyte
1 gigabyte=1000 megabytes.

A 3.5″ floppy disk will hold 1.44 megabytes (approximately twenty-five two-page typed documents, one or two high-quality digital pictures). A CD holds as much information as approximately 450 floppy disks!

Backup Making a duplicate copy of a file or a folder on a removable disk.

Select Highlighting a file, icon, word, or group of words by clicking your mouse.

Shortcut Usually refers to an icon on your desktop or programs menu. These icons go into your computer and find the item you are looking for . . . in other words, they *point* to a specific item and are not the actual item.

Clipboard Temporary storage of information that can be used in another computer program.

 **Cut** Removing part of a document to the clipboard.

 **Copy** Copying part of a document to the clipboard.

 **Paste** Placing the contents of the clipboard back into a document.

For a complete listing of technical terms and definitions, visit the following Web sites:

http://www.computerhope.com/jargon.htm

OR

http://www.Webopcdia.com/

Using the Start button

When you click on the START button you'll notice that it pops up a menu with about eight to ten different options.

The two most important options on this menu are:

1. The Programs menu, which lists all of the available software programs installed on your computer.
2. The Shutdown option, where you need to go *before* you shut your computer off.

The Programs menu is a long list of folders and individual icons representing the different programs installed on your computer.

With Windows 95/98, there are already many pre-installed icons and computer programs. These include the Accessories folder, which has items like your system tools, Internet tools, games, a calculator, a very basic word processor, a paint program, CD player and other utilities.

Each time you install a new program a corresponding folder and icons for that program will be installed in the programs menu.

Next to the Start button is a long gray bar known as the taskbar. At the end of the taskbar, you will find your system clock and some other smaller icons that represent certain programs that automatically start when Windows begins. To find out what these programs are, simply float your mouse over the icon (do not click); a label appears to identify the icon.

When using Microsoft Windows, it is extremely important to be familiar with the taskbar. On it, you will see that different buttons appear as you open and close different programs. It is designed to orient you to which programs are currently running and allow you to easily switch between them.

Starting a program

There are two ways to start a program.

The most common method:

1. Click on the START button
2. Click on PROGRAMS
3. Find and click on the desired program.

Another method is to double-click on an icon that exists on your desktop.

Program basics

There are three key areas that are identical to every "window" on every Window's program. Learning to recognize and understand these areas will make you more comfortable with the Windows environment and make it easier to learn new programs.

1. Pull Down Menu Bar

The pull down menu bar is a series of menus (activated with the click of a mouse) that contains all of the functions of a program.

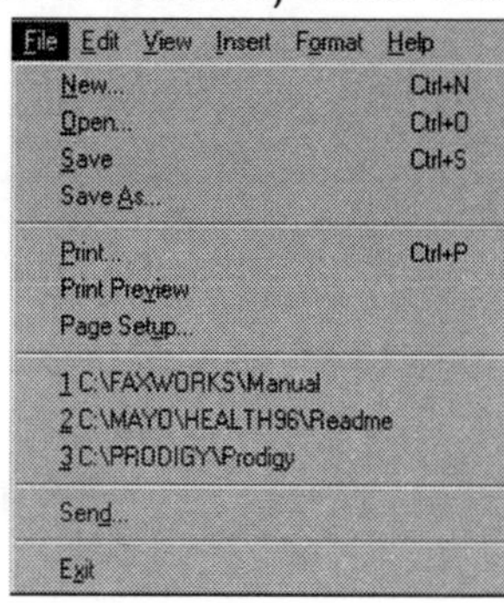

Tip within a tip:
When you learning a new program, it is good practice to click on every menu bar item and find out what lies in each of them.

2. Button or Tool Bar

Easy access to common functions such as print, save file, open file, font, cut, copy, paste, etc. Clicking on them with your mouse activates them. Also, if you hold your mouse pointer over a button (without clicking), the program will tell you what that particular button does.

3. Window Controls

These buttons are found in the upper right-hand corner of every window.

 This button will minimize or *shrink* your window to only a button on your taskbar.

 This button will enlarge your window to fit your entire screen or make your current window less than maximum.

 This button will exit the current program automatically. If you are working on a file that is not saved, the program will prompt you for more information.

How to delete unwanted icons from the desktop?

1. Click once on the unwanted icon.
2. Push delete on your key.

OR

1. Click and drag the unwanted icon to the RECYCLE BIN.

***Tip within a tip*:**
When you delete an icon from the desktop, you are not deleting the program, only the shortcut or pointer to the program.

How do I add an icon to the desktop?

If you are using Windows 98 or a newer version of Windows 95, try this:

1. Click on START.
2. Click on PROGRAMS.
3. Right click and drag the icon you want to add to your desktop.
4. Release the mouse button.
5. Click on the COPY HERE option from the menu that appears.

If you're using an earlier version of Windows 95, do this:

1. Click on START.
2. Click on SETTINGS.
3. Click on TASKBAR.
4. Click on START MENU PROGRAMS.
5. Click on ADVANCED.

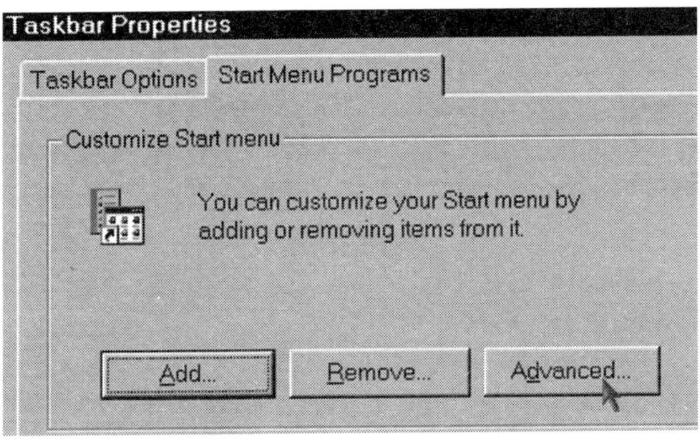

6. Click on the PROGRAMS folder in the left-handed section of this window.
7. Find the icon you would like to have on your desktop in the right-hand side of this window.

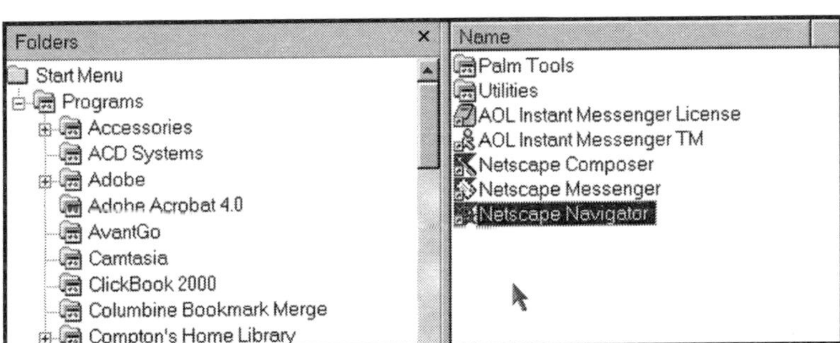

8. Right click on the icon you like to have on your desktop and drag the icon to your desktop .
9. Release the mouse button.
10. Click on the COPY HERE option from the menu that appears.

***Tip within a tip*:**

You can also create a shortcut on your desktop to a data file by:

1. Click on START → PROGRAMS.
2. Click on WINDOWS EXPLORER, find your data file and.
3. Right click and drag it to you desktop.
4. Release the button.
5. Click on CREATE SHORTCUT HERE from the menu that pops up.

Using the taskbar (multi-tasking)

Earlier in this section, I alluded to the fact that the taskbar was an important area for you to be aware of during your computing. Here is a tutorial of how the taskbar works.

1. Close any open programs you have on your computer.
2. Note that your taskbar is now blank (with the exception of the small icons next to your clock).
3. Click on START.
4. Click on PROGRAMS.

5. Click on ACCESSORIES.
6. Click on GAMES.
7. Click on SOLITAIRE.
   - ➲ Note now that you have a button on your taskbar that says Solitaire.

8. Click on START.
9. Click on PROGRAMS.
10. Click on ACCESSORIES.
11. Click on NOTEPAD.
    - ➲ Note now that you have an button not only for Solitaire, but also for the Notepad on your taskbar.

12. Click on START.
13. Click on PROGRAMS.
14. Click on ACCESSORIES.
15. Click on WORDPAD.
    - ➲ Now you will notice that there are three buttons on the taskbar; Solitaire, Notepad, and WordPad.

16. The WordPad window is the current window you are looking at now.
17. Click one time on the SOLITAIRE button on the taskbar.
18. Now the Solitaire window is the window that came forward (you may notice the WordPad window behind this one).
19. Click one time on the NOTEPAD button on the taskbar.
20. Now the Notepad window is the window that came forward.

This simple exercise demonstrates that you can have more than one activity going at the same time with Microsoft Windows.

In other words, Windows allows you to keep programs open that you refer to often such as calendar programs or other reference material as you are composing letters or word processing or surfing the Internet and writing email.

The taskbar tracks these activities for you and allows you to switch among these activities simply by pushing the corresponding button to the activity you want to bring forward as you just finished doing.

***Tip within a tip*:**
On most computers, you can safely run up to six different programs at the same time. The number can be higher or lower depending on how much RAM you have installed on your computer and the programs being run.

How do I install a new program?

New program installation has come a long way and is mostly automated today. However, in order to avoid problems with installation, follow these steps.

Before buying a new program, read the box and find out what the minimum requirements are to run the program. Every software package will tell you how much memory, hard drive space, version of Windows and other system requirements you need in order to run the program. Your computer should meet these minimum requirements before you purchase the program.

Before inserting the CD to install the new program, you need to shut down all programs you may be running on your computer. Shut down computer programs by:

1. Push Control+Alt+Delete on your keyboard all at the same time (this will invoke the close program dialog box).

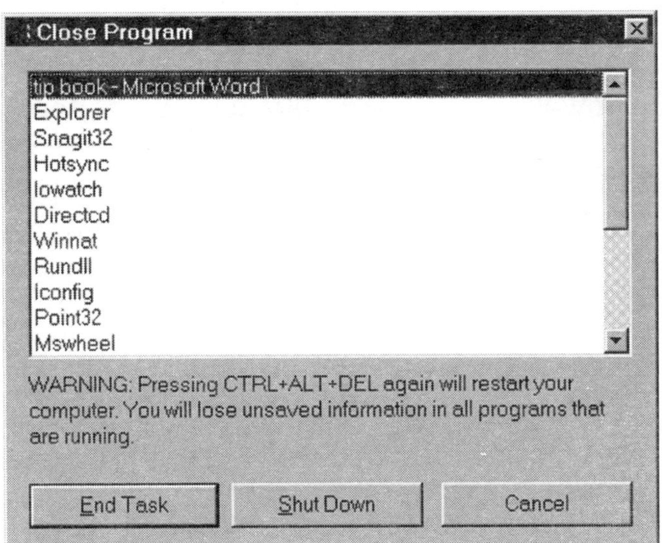

2. In this window, you will note that there are many cryptic words in the white box . . .

some you will recognize some you won't. These programs are small utilities and Windows system programs that start automatically each time you start your computer. In order to perform a "clean" installation of your new program, you need to close all but two of these programs.

3. The only two programs in this list that will be remaining when we are done with this procedure are Explorer and Systray.
4. Click one time on any of the other programs and then click on the END TASK button.
5. Push Control+Alt+Delete on your keyboard again to invoke the Close Program dialog box again.
6. Click one time on any of the programs in the list and then click END TASK.
7. Repeat this process until only Explorer and Systray remain.**
8. Now you can insert your new computer program CD and follow the instructions that came with the program (or instructions that appear on-screen).

Note: Occasionally you will see a pop-up window telling you that a program is "not responding." Click on the END TASK button and proceed.

After installation is complete, if the program does not ask you to restart the computer, restart your computer to restore programs closed for installation by:

1. Click on START.
2. Click on SHUT DOWN.
3. Click on RESTART.

4. Click on the OK button.

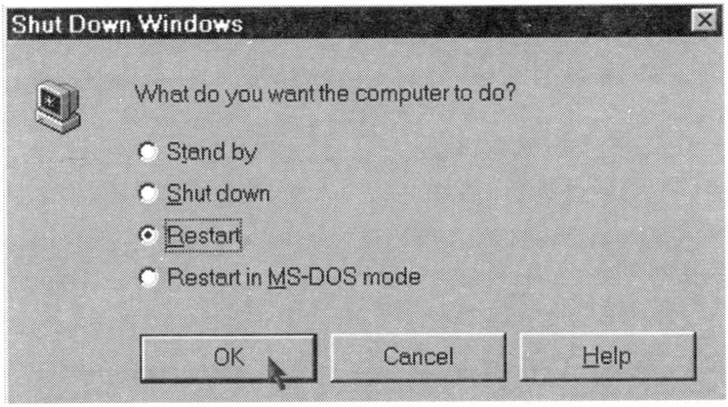

How do I delete an entire program?

Deleting files on your computer can become a harrowing experience if you accidentally delete a file vital to your computer's health, so use one of these two methods to clean up unwanted programs.

1. Click on START.
2. Click on PROGRAMS.
3. Find the program you would like to delete and look for an uninstall or remove option in its group.

If you cannot find an uninstall or remove option in the programs group, then try this:

1. Click on START.
2. Click on SETTINGS.
3. Click on CONTROL PANEL.
4. Double-click on ADD/REMOVE PROGRAMS
5. Scroll through the list of programs in this list and click on the program you want to remove.
6. Click on the ADD/REMOVE button.

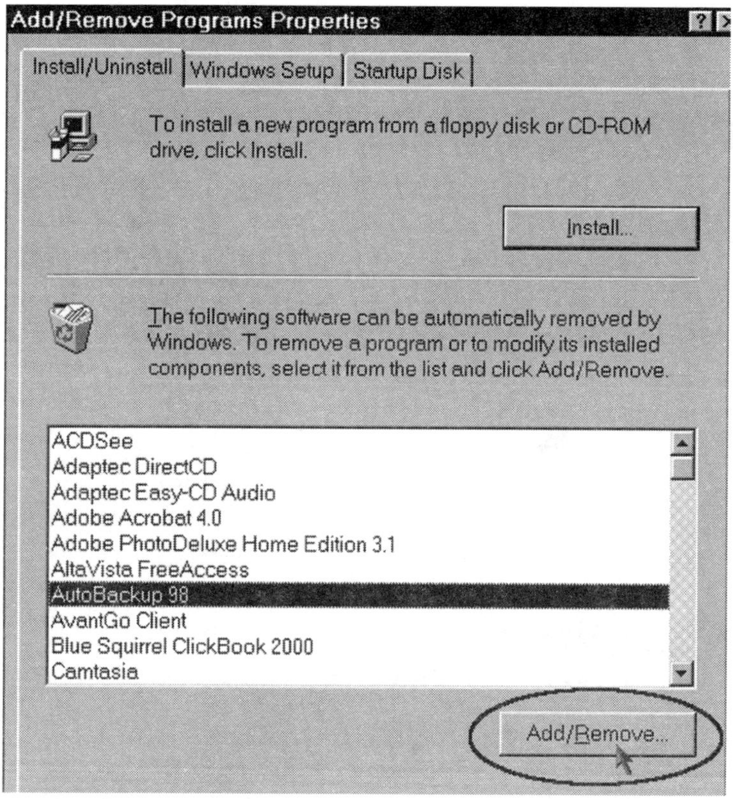

These are the two best methods of deleting an unwanted program from your computer. Unless you are very well versed with a computer, do *not*

attempt deleting programs any other way without help.

Deleting individual files

There are only two rules to abide by when deleting files:

1. Delete only files that you have created or downloaded (i.e. word processor files, scans, downloaded pictures, etc.).
2. Do NOT empty the RECYCLE BIN for *at least* two full computer sessions after deleting files . . . this will give you a safety net in case you accidentally deleted a needed file.

The act of deleting a file is dangerously easy:

1. Find the file you want to delete either through WINDOWS EXPLORER or MY COMPUTER.
2. Click ONE time on it.
3. Push delete on your keyboard.
4. Answer yes to the question about sending it to the RECYCLE BIN.

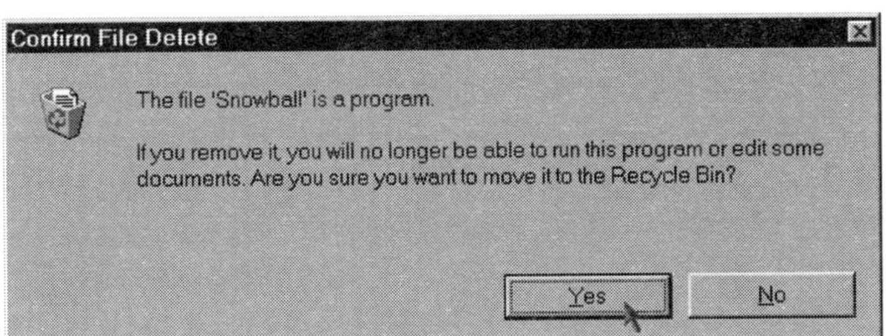

Recovering a deleted file

1. Double-click on your RECYCLE BIN on the desktop.
2. Find the file you want to recover.
3. Right click on it.
4. Click on RESTORE.
5. The file will be restored to its original location.

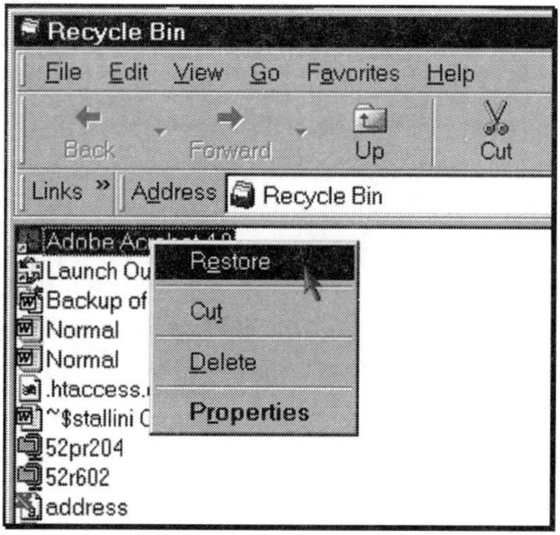

Emptying your RECYCLE BIN

When you are sure that you don't need your deleted files anymore, empty your recycle bin by:

1. Right click on the RECYCLE BIN.
2. Click on EMPTY RECYCLE BIN.
3. Click on YES.

Tip within a Tip:
The RECYCLE BIN acts a safety net for files you accidentally delete. Only empty your RECYCLE BIN about once a month and only when you know there are no files you really need.

Keeping track of your computer storage

Following these steps, you can easily keep track of how much space you have on your computer for new documents and programs.

1. Double-click on the MY COMPUTER icon on your desktop.
2. Right click on your hard drive (labeled C).
3. Click on PROPERTIES

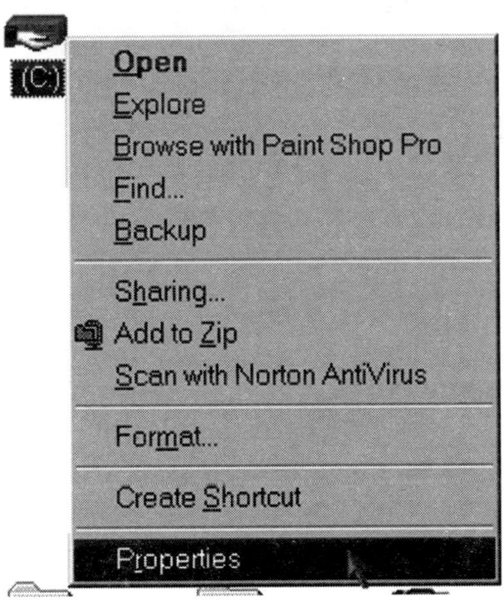

4. An easy to read pie chart informs you how much free space and how much empty space you have on your computer.

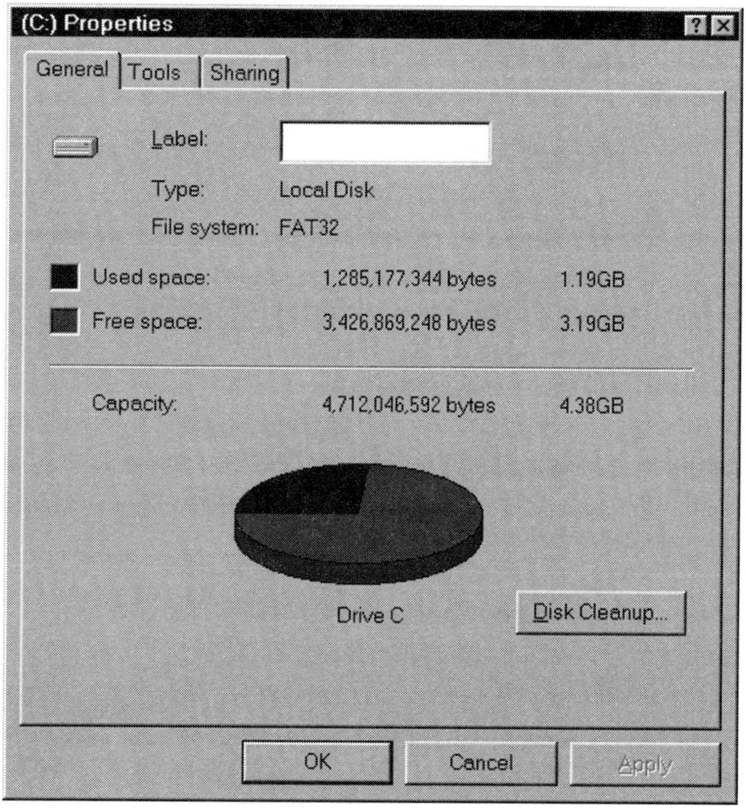

Tip within a tip:
Your free space should be equal to or greater than twice the amount of RAM you have on your computer (example: 32 megabytes of RAM = 64 megabytes or greater of free hard drive space).

Tip within a tip within a tip:
This technique works for Zip, floppy and CDR/RW disks as well.

Font management

Fonts are the different typefaces that we can choose when we create word processing documents, newsletters and other computer-generated documents.

I am willing to wager that most computer users only use about a dozen different fonts. However, there are more than 400 different fonts installed on many computers today.

These fonts utilize precious computer memory resources and also increase computer boot time. Here is how to better manage your fonts so that you can release some of your computer resources and decrease the time your computer takes to boot up.

To view how many fonts and what types of fonts are on your computer currently, follow these steps:

1. Click on START.
2. Click on SETTINGS.
3. Click on CONTROL PANEL.
4. Double-click on FONTS.

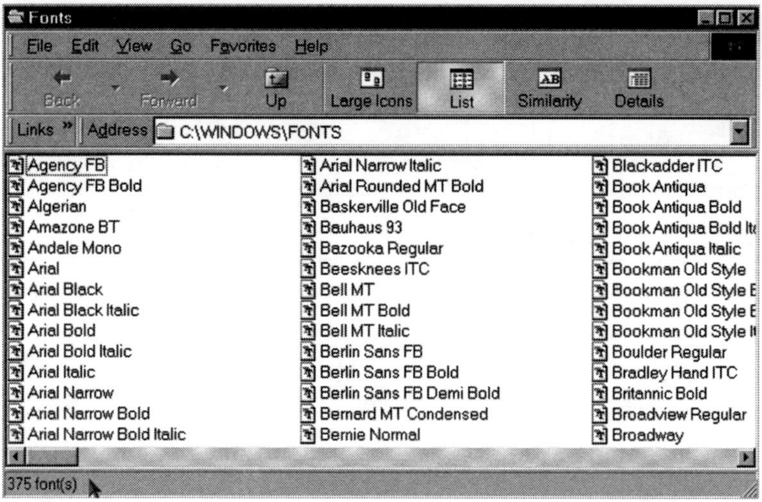

In this window, you will be able to see all the fonts that are installed on your computer and how many fonts are installed on your computer by looking at the bottom of the window.

You can preview any of these fonts by double-clicking on the font name, but to delete them you will have to close that preview window and then delete the font from the list.

An easier way to manage fonts is to use a font utility program. My favorite font utility program is called ***Font Lister***.

Font Lister is a very small utility that allows you to not only see the list of fonts on your system, but you can also preview them very easily with your own custom text, delete unwanted fonts, and a print a copy of all your fonts for visual reference.

You will notice that many of the fonts on your system look alike. Pick out your favorites and then delete the rest.

Font Lister can be downloaded free from: http://www.theill.com/fl/

Navigating a save or open dialog box

These are the windows that open when you want to save a new file or open an old one. Learning to navigate and understand them takes practice, but pays big dividends in your computing life.

1. From any Windows program, click on FILE from the menus at the top of the screen.
2. Click on SAVE AS.
3. You will now be presented with the following screen.

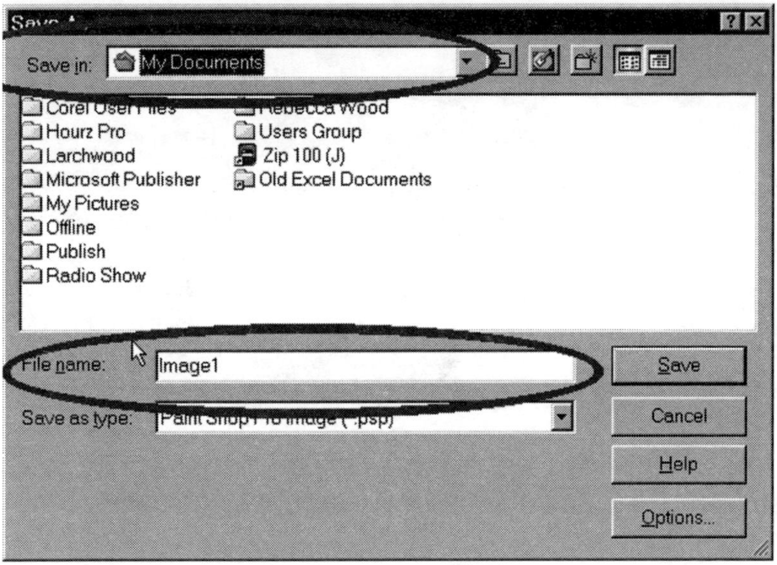

4. There is a lot on the screen, however, you need only concern yourself with two areas right now (the ones circled).
5. The first place you want to be aware of is the SAVE IN box at the top of the screen. This is the folder where your work will be saved. Usually you will accept the default location, but you can choose any folder you wish.
6. The next place is the FILE NAME box. Type the name of your document (file) here. It can include spaces and up to 256 characters.
7. Click on the SAVE button.

When you want to open saved work, you will click on FILE and then OPEN from any program and will be presented with this same screen.

File management

File management and the discussion of files and folders may not be terribly interesting, but a little knowledge of the subject will pay large dividends as you embark on this technology journey.

More definitions

Files	Information that you created or a computer program created that is stored on your computer and has a name. (Example: a résumé, spreadsheet or scanned picture).
Folders	Part of your computer that organizes your files by category. (Example: My Documents, Program Files, Windows, etc.) Folders also have names that describe what type of files it contains.

Note in the next diagram (a picture of Windows Explorer . . . a program in Windows where you manage your files and folders), that all your folders reside on the left-hand side of the screen.

Windows Explorer is accessed by clicking on:
START → PROGRAMS → WINDOWS EXPLORER

If you click on anyone of the folders on the left, its ***contents*** are viewable on the right. In the screen shot on the next picture, the folder named Radio

Show is highlighted and its contents are viewable on the right. The contents can include subfolders. **Important**: Do NOT delete any files or folders that you did not create. Deleting files that you are not aware of their origins can cause serious problems to your computer.

From Windows Explorer (pictured below) and any save file dialog box (see the following two tips), you can delete, rename, backup and move files or folders.

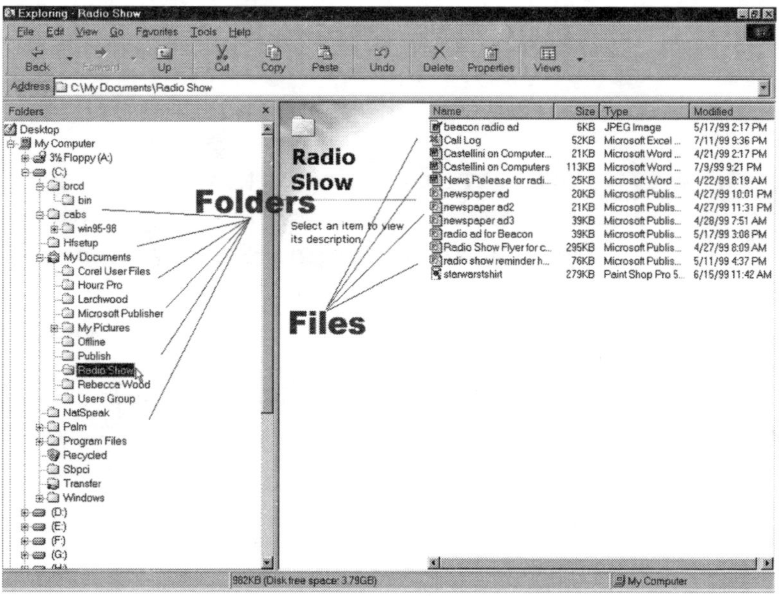

Note also in this picture that some Folders have a **+** sign next to them. That indicates that they contain other folders or what is known as a subfolder. Subfolders are used to further organize your files.

Easy file management

You can easily delete and rename files from within almost any computer program.

To delete a file:

1. Click on FILE from the menus.
2. Click on OPEN.
3. In the window that pops up, click ONCE on any document you want to delete.
4. Push DELETE on your keyboard. Repeat as many times as you need would like.

To rename a file:

1. Click on FILE from the menu of any program.
2. Click on OPEN.
3. Click ONCE on the file you want to rename.
4. Click ONCE more on the name of the file and you should get your blinking cursor allowing you to rename the file.

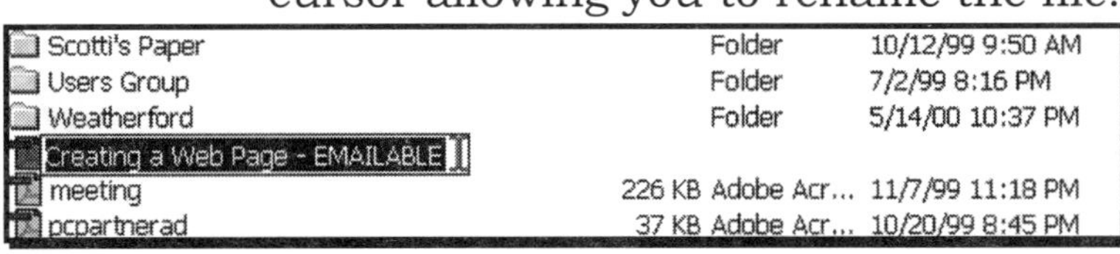

5. After renaming the file, push ENTER on your keyboard.

NOTE: To perform these operations, the file cannot be currently open.

Easy file management Part II

Backup and organize your files from the same dialog box (FILE → OPEN) that we used in the previous tip.

First, when you save your files, you should always be paying attention to the top of the save window where the computer shows you ***where the file is being saved***.

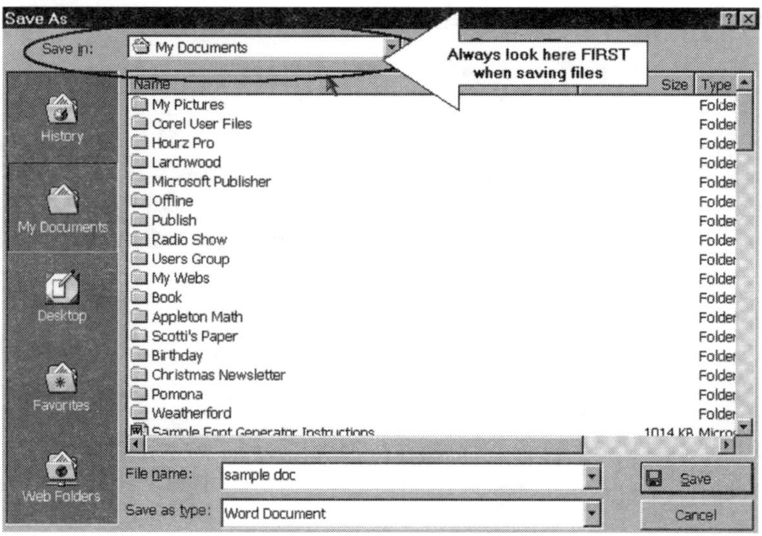

You can organize your saving further by moving your eye to the right a little and noticing the *new folder* icon (pictured).

When you click on this icon, a new folder is created in the contents part of the window in the middle of the window. Type a name for your new folder and then press enter on your keyboard. Now double-click on that folder to save files in it.

Backing up files from the Save or Open dialog box in any program, provides a convenient opportunity for backing up your files.

1. Right click on any file or folder in the contents area and then
2. Click on SEND TO → 3½″ FLOPPY DISK.

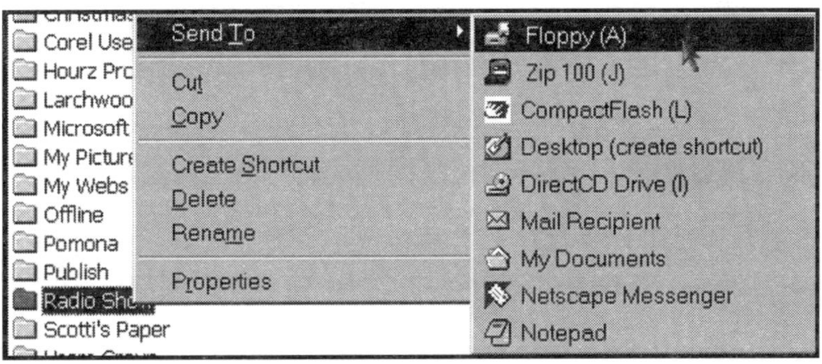

***Tip within a tip*:**
You can also use this method to send files directly to a CDR/CDRW drive or Zip drive.

Create a new toolbar in Windows

Desktop icons provide easy access commonly used programs. However, you may not like twenty or more icons on your desktop.

Using Windows toolbars provides an even better way to access those commonly used programs and keep the desktop a little cleaner at the same time.

After following the outlined steps below*, you will have an orderly toolbar that contains easy one-click access to your favorite programs or files:

1. Drag icons of your favorite programs from your desktop or the START → PROGRAMS menu to the toolbar that is sitting right next to your START button (the one with the Internet Explorer icon and show desktop icon). HINT: Drag the icons with your RIGHT mouse button so that you can copy the icon instead of moving it.

2. You won't immediately see all the icons that you have placed here, but don't despair.

3. Now, position your mouse over the little raised bar that is between this toolbar and your START button (your cursor should now look like an arrow pointing left and right).

4. Click and drag this toolbar towards your desktop and it will move the toolbar off of the taskbar to make its own separate toolbox called Quick Launch.

5. I suggest now dragging the toolbar (by clicking on the title bar of the Window . . . see picture) to either side or top of your screen to "dock" it and have it out of the way.

6. One last step, right click on a blank part of the new toolbar and click on the ALWAYS ON TOP option (if it is not already checked) so that it is visible in whatever program you might be using.

   - To delete items from your new toolbar, right click on the icon and then click on delete from the menu.

   - Add new items by simply dragging them to the toolbar.

Now you can see all of your commonly used files and programs at a glance and just click on them once to access them . . . pretty handy.

**You have to be using Windows 98 or Me or Windows 95 with Internet Explorer 4.0 or greater installed in order to take advantage of this tip.*

Speaking of the desktop

You can quickly return to your desktop without closing your current program(s) by clicking on the SHOW DESKTOP icon.

Move your START button back to the bottom of the screen

Occasionally you may find that your START button and taskbar have moved from their default position to either of the sides or top of the screen.

Here's how to move them back to the bottom of your screen (or if you *want* to move it, this will work for you as well).

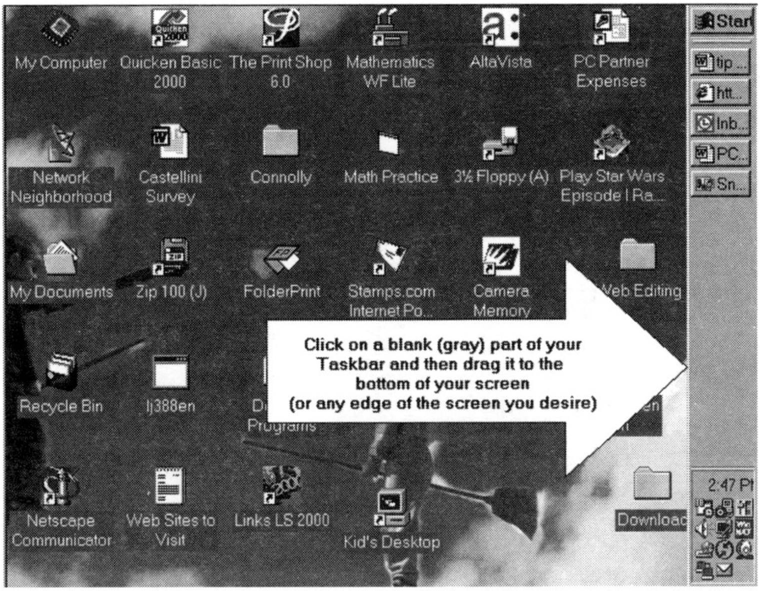

1. Click and hold your mouse button on any blank (gray) part of the taskbar.
2. Drag the bar to any edge of the screen (you will not see the taskbar coming with you, but you will see a light outline at the edge of the screen you moved to when the mouse is properly positioned).
3. Let go of the mouse button and now you have taskbar back where you want it.

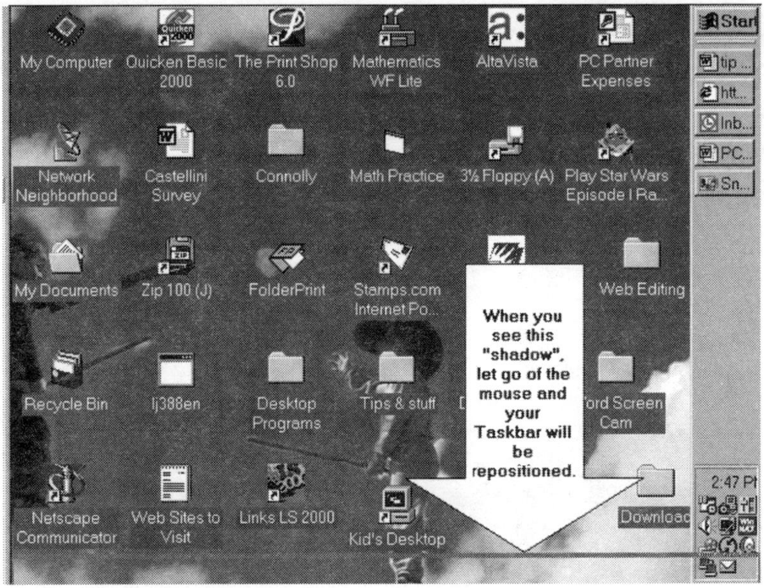

Make your taskbar disappear

If you have a small screen or just don't want to always be looking at your taskbar, try this:

1. Click on START.
2. Click on SETTINGS.
3. Click on TASKBAR.
4. Check the box that's marked AUTO HIDE.
5. Click on OK.

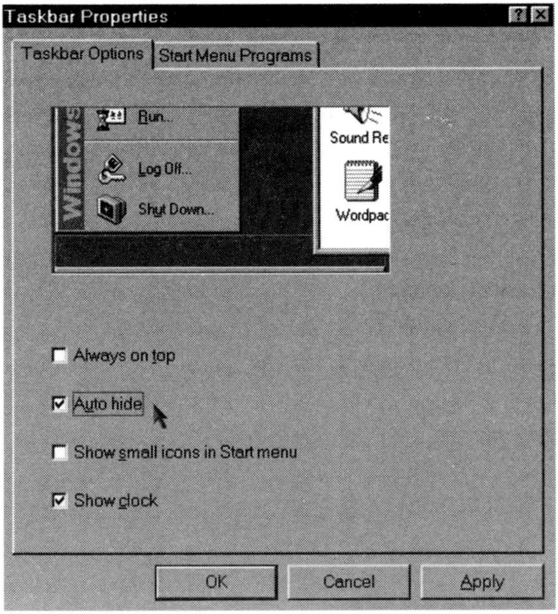

To view your taskbar, just move your mouse to the bottom of your screen and it will pop up.

Create a desktop shortcut

Do you get tired of looking through the programs menu for your favorite program? Then learn how to put an icon (shortcut) to your favorite program on your desktop.

NOTE: This tip applies to Windows 98 (and Me) and Windows 95 with Internet Explorer 4.0 or later installed.

1. Click on START.
2. Click on PROGRAMS.
3. Navigate to your favorite program, then . . .

4. Right click and drag the program to your desktop.

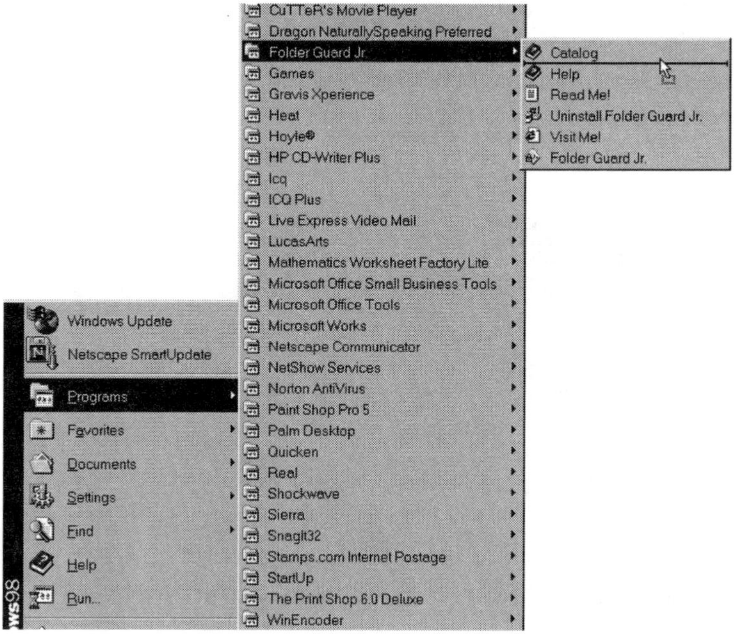

5. When you release the mouse button, click on the COPY HERE option from the resulting menu.

You can place as many icons on your desktop as you desire.

***Tip within a tip*:**
To delete an unwanted icon from your desktop, simply drag it to your recycle bin.

Backup, backup, backup!

The worst scenario a computer user can face is the loss of important data such as a family history, important spreadsheet or financial files, schoolwork, etc.

It doesn't take long to back up your files, but it does take discipline. Just like getting the oil changed in our cars regularly to maintain its health, it is imperative that a good backup program be put in place for you computer creations.

Follow these simple rules for backing up your files and you will be able to face any computer calamity:

- Save your files in a common folder or directory (make subfolders if you have a lot of categories).
- You do NOT need to back up the entire hard disk. Most of the hard disk is occupied by program files not your data files and program files can be restored from the original CDs.
- Open Windows Explorer (START → PROGRAMS → WINDOWS EXPLORER), find

the folder that you are saving your data files in and right click on it. Now click on SEND TO, then 3½″ FLOPPY DISK (or CDR/RW or Zip Drive).

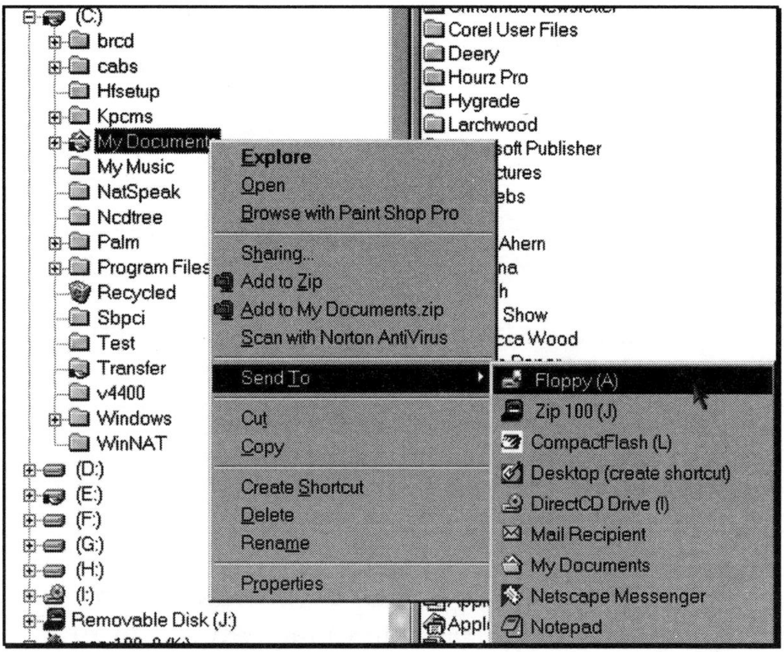

That's it! The entire contents of your important folder will be transferred to a floppy disk (if there is more information in the folder than can fit on a single floppy, the computer will prompt you for another disk).

Other important considerations:

- Take advantage of the built-in backup programs that come with all financial software (usually accessed through the File menu).

- Make at least two backup copies of everything you deem important.
- If you have extremely critical data, then consider keeping one of your backups onsite and take another backup to a bank safe deposit box or some other safe place.
- Backup your data at least monthly and more often if you create or modify data files often.
- If you use a digital camera or scanner frequently, you will need to consider a Zip drive or recordable CD to archive and backup these larger files.

Stopping the starting

Are you having a tough time figuring out how to keep some programs from automatically opening every time Windows starts? Then this tip is for you.

First, start by looking in the preference or options of the problematic program. Often you will find a simple check box that allows you to disable the *auto start* feature.

If you have no luck with that method, then try one of these options:

If you are using Windows 98, then the method is easier than with Windows 95:

1. Click on START.
2. Click on PROGRAMS.
3. Click on ACCESSORIES.
4. Click on SYSTEM TOOLS.
5. Click on SYSTEM INFORMATION.
6. Click on the TOOLS menu.
7. Click on SYSTEM CONFIGURATION UTILITY (or you can get here by clicking on START → RUN → type: msconfig and press enter on your keyboard).
8. Click on the STARTUP tab.

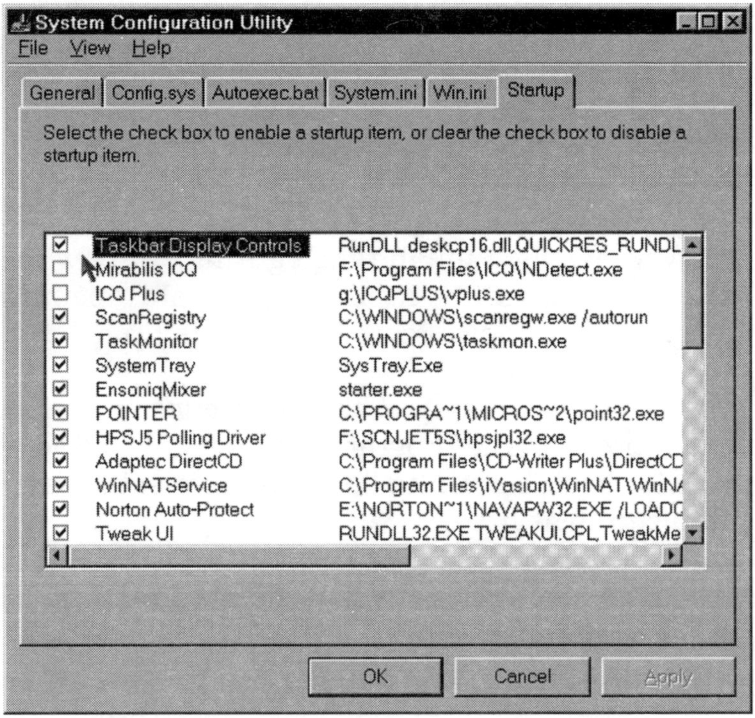

9. Now scroll through the list of programs that are automatically starting, and uncheck the box next to them.
10. Click OK twice and restart your computer.

If you are using Windows 95, try this:

1. Click on START.
2. Click on SETTINGS.
3. Click on TASKBAR AND START MENU.
4. Click on the START MENU PROGRAMS tab at the top of the screen.
5. Click on the REMOVE button.

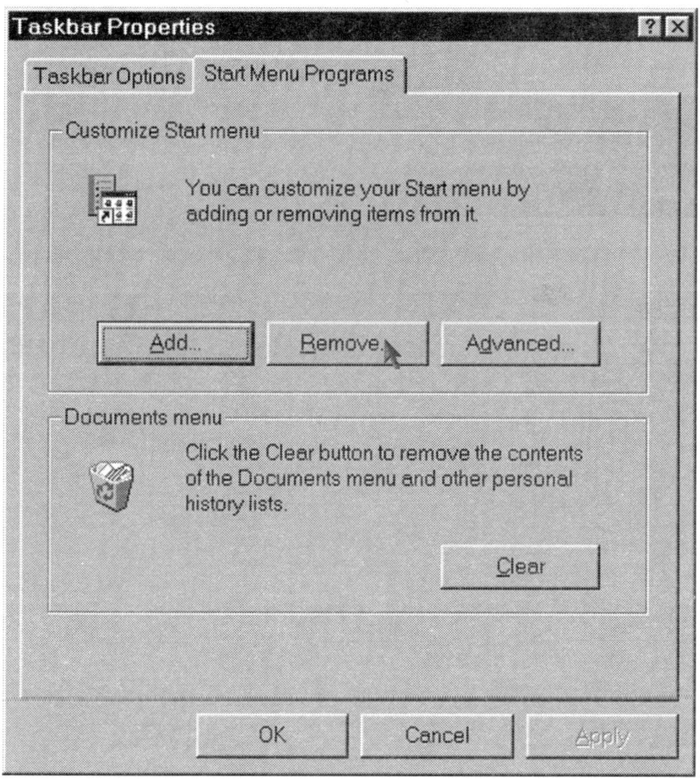

6. Scroll through the list and click on the plus sign next to the STARTUP FOLDER.

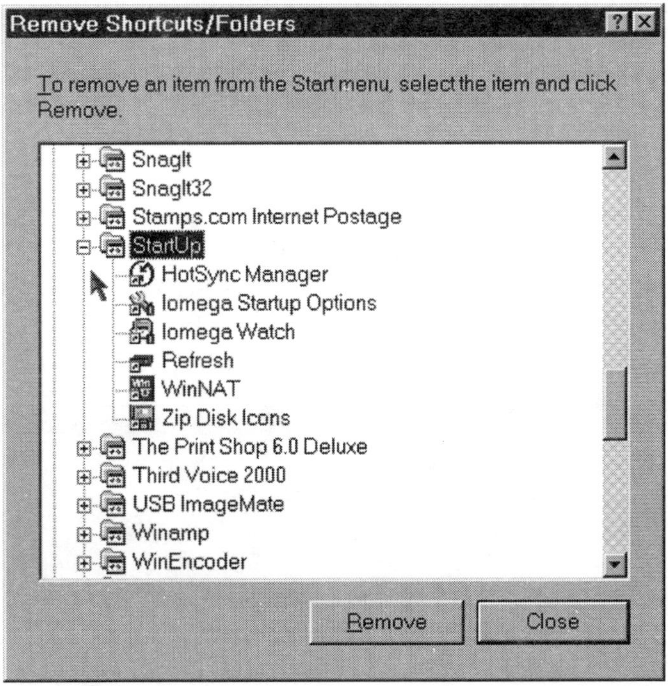

7. Click on the program that you don't want to start and then click on the REMOVE button.
8. Repeat the last step for all the programs you want to prevent from automatically starting.
9. Click on CLOSE.
10. Click on OK.

Photo wallpaper

If you own a scanner or digital camera, here is a simple technique to turn your favorite photo into wallpaper for your computer (the background to your desktop):

Windows 98

1. Save your favorite photo in JPEG or BMP format to the Windows folder.
2. Right click on the DESKTOP.
3. Click on PROPERTIES.
4. Scroll through the list to find your newly saved photo and click on it.

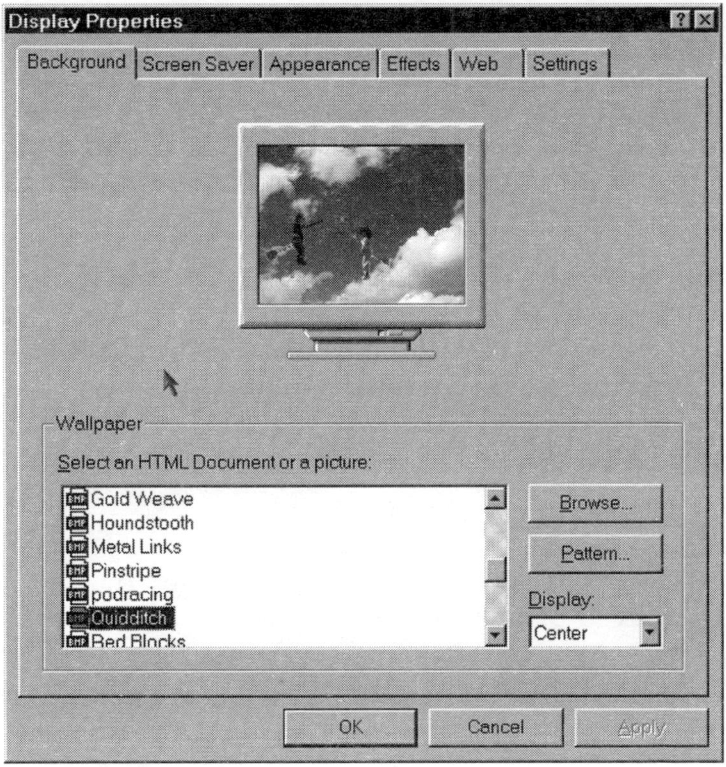

5. Click on OK.

Windows 95

The technique is exactly the same as above, except that you must save your photo in BMP format. Windows 95 does not recognize the JPEG format for wallpaper.

Instant shut down

This tip requires strict attention to detail. If you do not feel comfortable with the process, do not attempt it.

1. Right click on a blank portion of your desktop.
2. Click on NEW.
3. Click on SHORTCUT.
4. Type:

C:\windows\rundll.exe user.exe,exitwindows

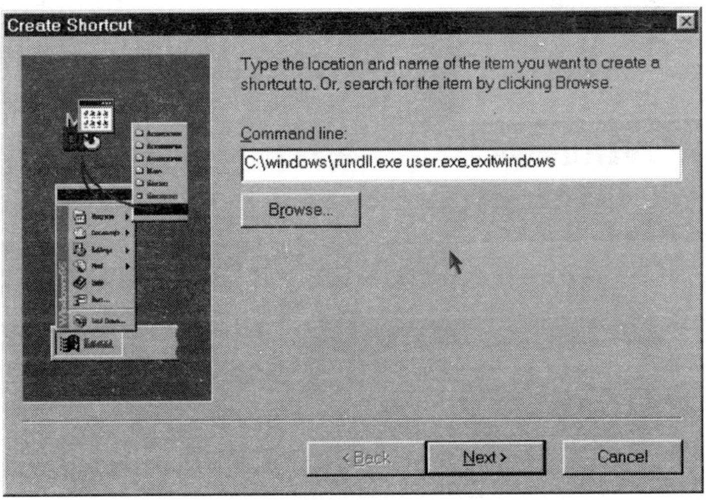

5. Click NEXT.
6. Type: Shut Down My Computer
7. Click FINISH.

Now to use it, simply double-click on the new shortcut and your computer will shut down.

Automatically starting favorite programs

We discussed how to *stop* certain programs from automatically starting in Windows. To have a program start automatically, use this technique.

For example, you may want your computer to automatically open and check for email in the morning when you turn on your computer. Or, maybe you have a daily routine with your *Quicken* that you complete first thing and you would like the program to be up and running immediately. Here's how:

Windows 98 (or Windows 95 *with* Internet Explorer 4 or greater)

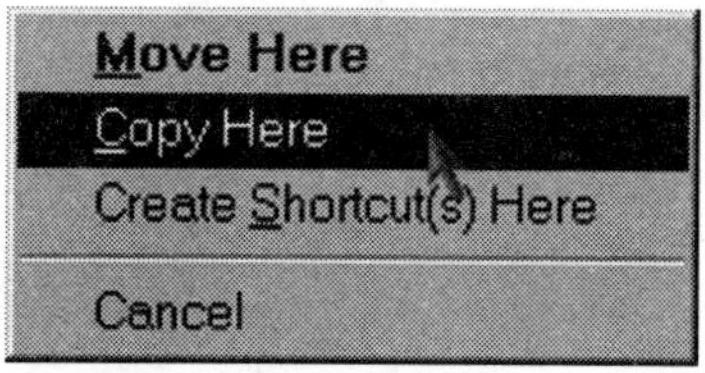

1. Click on START.
2. Click on PROGRAMS.
3. Right click and drag the program that you want to start automatically to the Startup folder.
4. Release the button and click on the COPY HERE option.
5. Repeat process for other programs you want to load automatically.

Windows 95

1. Click on START.
2. Click on SETTINGS.
3. Click on TASKBAR.
4. Click on the START MENU PROGRAMS tab at the top of the screen.
5. Click on ADVANCED.
6. Find the program icon that you want to automatically start.
7. Right click on it.
8. Click on COPY from the menu.
9. Right click on the STARTUP folder.
10. Click on PASTE.
11. Repeat for any other programs that you want to automatically load.

When you reboot your computer, the program(s) you placed into the Startup folder will automatically start.

Windows key shortcuts

Have you ever wondered what that little Windows key (between the Ctrl and Alt keys on most keyboards) does?

Wonder no more:

- Windows Key + E = Windows Explorer
- Windows Key + F = Find Function
- Windows Key + R = Run Function

- Windows Key + M = Minimize all open windows so that you can see your desktop again. (Windows Key + D will do the same thing.)
- Windows Key + C = Control Panel
- Windows Key + Pause/Break = System Properties
- Windows Key + P = Printers Folder
- Shift+Windows Key + M = Undo minimize all windows
- Windows Key + K = opens Keyboard properties
- Windows Key + I = open Mouse Properties

Printing out error messages*

We all have computer mishaps and end up having to call for help. One of the first questions the helper (tech support) always asks is, "What was the message you received?"

Most of the time, in our frustration, we failed to write down the content of the message. Here is a tip that will bypass the writing altogether and allow you to answer that first question from your digital helper.

When an error occurs follow these steps:

1. **Before** clicking on the OK or CANCEL button on the error message press the PRINT SCREEN button on your keyboard (located above the delete, and home keys in the middle of your keyboard).

2. Close the error message.
3. Open up your favorite word processing software (Word, Works, WordPerfect, etc.).
4. Click on EDIT.
5. Click on PASTE.
6. A picture of your computer screen (with the pesky error window) will appear.
7. Click on FILE.
8. Click on PRINT.

No writing or fumbling for paper, simply press a few keystrokes and you have a nice clean printout of your mistakes.

Note: This tip will not work with the infamous *Blue Screen of Death* or if the computer freezes.

Internet, Email and More

Arguably, the most exciting advance in modern-day computers has been the proliferation of the Internet. In this section, you will learn how to:

- navigate the Internet quickly
- organize your findings on the Internet
- search the Internet effectively
- print information that you want to keep for later reference
- and much more!

Internet or Web addresses

When you sign up for the Internet, you are given a software package called the browser that allows you to view the content that is available via the Internet. The browsers discussed in this section are Netscape Communicator (4.0 and greater), Internet Explorer (4.0 and greater) and America Online (4.0 and greater).

The content, of which I speak is available via the Internet, comprises more than one billion pages of information accessible from your computer. These pages are called Web sites. A Web site is identified via a unique address.

A Web site address follows this format:

http://www.yahoo.com
http://www.usatoday.com
http://www.yourpcpartner.com

Note how all Web sites start with the beginning of HTTP. However, many times when you see a company or organization advertising its Web site, the advertisement will leave out the HTTP portion of the Web site address.

Tip within a tip:
Sometimes you will see or hear a Web address referred to as an URL (pronounced "earl"). That's short for Uniform Resource Locator. It's a five-dollar word for Web site address.

Quickly navigating to a Web site

Follow this tip to get to a Web site that you hear advertised on the radio or TV or read in an ad or on a business card.

When on the Internet, look toward the top of your screen and look for a long white box with an "http://" address in it (pictured below)

This is called the browser address or location bar. You will interact with it to successfully complete this tip.

Netscape Communicator

1. Click once in the long white "location" box at the top of your screen (this will highlight any text that is already in the box).
2. Type in the address *without the http://*
3. Make sure that you have no extra spaces in the address, and that the spelling is accurate.
4. Press enter on your keyboard.
5. The Web site will now load into your window.
6. Repeat this process for any Web site address that you happen to see on a TV commercial, newspaper or magazine ad, billboard or any other means.

Internet Explorer

1. Click once in the long white "address" box at the top of your screen (this will highlight any text that is already in the box).
2. Type in the address without the http://
3. Make sure they you have no extra spaces in the address, and that the spelling is accurate.
4. Press enter on your keyboard.
5. The Web site will now load into your window.
6. Repeat this process for any Web site address that you happen to see on a TV commercial, newspaper or magazine ad, billboard or any other means.

America Online version 4 or greater (AOL)

1. Click once in the long white GO box at the top of your screen (this will highlight any text that is already in the box).
2. Type in the address without the http://
3. Make sure they you have no extra spaces in the address and that the spelling is accurate.
4. Press enter on your keyboard.
5. The Web site will now load into your window.
6. Repeat this process for any Web site address that you happen to see on a TV commercial, newspaper or magazine ad, billboard or any other means.

No more complicated than these three steps. Just make sure that your spelling is correct and that you use periods instead of commas.

***Tip within a tip*:**
Note that in step 2, I did not say you have to push delete on your keyboard to clear the address already there.

When text is highlighted (as in step 1), anything you type replaces the highlighted text. No need to push backspace or delete on your keyboard.

Tip within a tip within a tip:
This technique holds true anywhere you highlight text . . . word processors, spreadsheets, etc. Just highlight and type!

Ignore the ads

Web pages contain numerous images, pictures, scrolling text, articles and other pieces of information.

For someone new to the Internet, it can almost be as much sensory overload as visiting the Las Vegas Strip.

The Internet succeeds at flashing advertisements at users. In fact, newer Internet users tend to have their eyes drawn to the billboard type advertisements (called banner ads) at the top of many Web pages rather than at the content of the Web page they were looking for.

Banner ads and their sponsors subsidize much of the Internet for us, so I don't despise the ads. Just be aware that they are there and quickly move to your targeted information unless you are truly interested in the banner.

After visiting a few Web sites, you will become accustomed to filtering out the extraneous information on a Web page and quickly finding information you are looking for.

What is a home page?

Let's back up for just a second to explore a couple of other terms. Each *screen* of information that you view on the Internet is considered a Web page.

A Web site contains many (thousands in some cases) of Web pages.

The first page of a Web site is known as the home page. When a company advertises its Web site, the address you see is its home page because its address is short and easy to remember.

For example, here are two Web pages from the Yahoo! Web site.

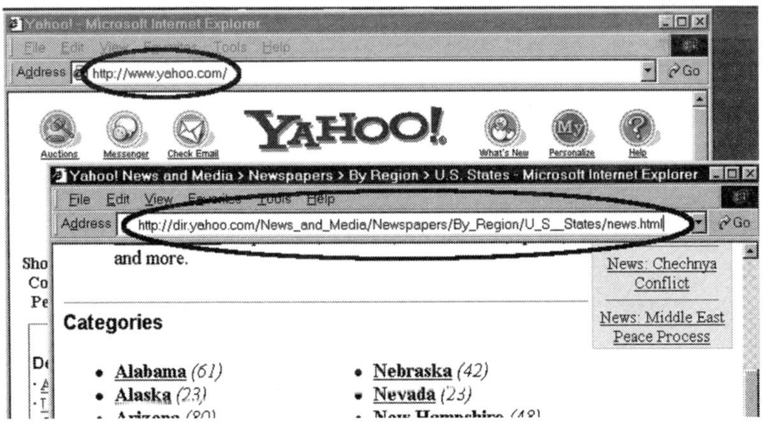

The bottom window is Yahoo!'s *home page* or the first page of the massive Web site. Notice that the Web site address is the one it advertises:

www.yahoo.com

The window on top is a Web page that you get to by clicking on many links from within the site. Note its long address.

Links and hyperlinks

When you are viewing a Web page, you will find many words that are underlined and usually blue in color, these are known as links or hyperlinks (see the previous picture).

When you move your mouse over one of these links, you'll notice that your mouse pointer turns from an arrow to a small hand. You will also notice that your mouse will change to a small hand over certain pictures or graphics on a Web page.

This change in your mouse cursor indicates that you have come across a *link* that will take you to a different page or set of information when you clicked on it.

Links and navigating around Internet are no more mysterious than that. Look through a particular page and when you see something interesting, click your mouse on it to be instantly provided with more information about your particular topic.

***Tip within a tip*:**
If you are using Internet Explorer 4.0 or greater, you can hold down the SHIFT key on your keyboard as you are clicking on a link and the link will open in a separate window . . . very handy for searching.

If you are using AOL or Netscape Communicator, you can right click on a link and then click on OPEN IN A NEW WINDOW from the pop-up menu to perform the same action.

Moving around the Internet

Much like you use your remote control on your TV to move forward and backward through different channels, the BACK and FORWARD buttons on your Internet browser to do the same thing.

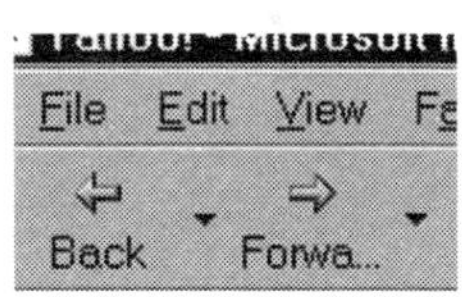

➲ Click on the BACK button and you will be transported *back* to the last Web page you visited.

➲ Click on the FORWARD button and move forward one Web page again.

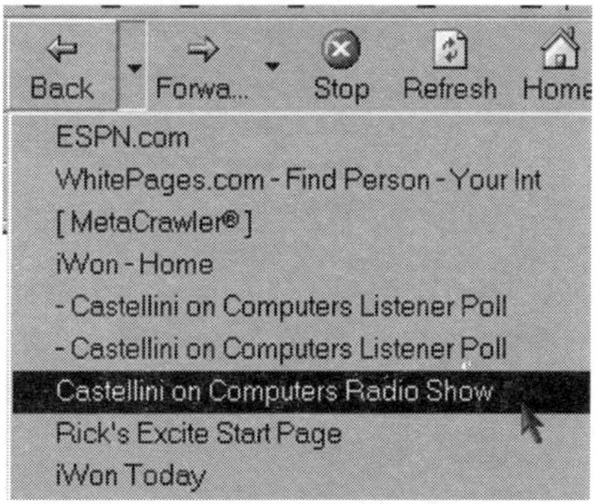

Tip within a tip:
If you click and hold your mouse button down on a BACK or FORWARD button in Netscape Communicator 4.0 or greater or Internet Explorer 4.0 or greater, a list of all the Web pages you visited in this particular session will be available for you to quickly navigate back to or forward to.

Sorry AOL users, your browser does not support this feature.

Tip within a tip:
AOL users, don't despair, you can use Netscape or Internet Explorer by:

1. Log onto AOL as normal.
2. Minimize AOL using the minimize button in the upper right-hand corner. 
3. Double click on your choice of Netscape or Internet Explorer.

Home, stop and refresh

These three buttons are native to all browsers.

- **Stop** allows you to stop further download of a page. For example, if you reach a Web site where you just want to read the text and don't care about the pictures, you can click on STOP and the graphics will stop loading.

- **Refresh** (called Reload in Netscape)—use this button when you are on a Web site where the information changes frequently such as weather or stock quotes. If you have been viewing the page for a length of time, clicking on this button will *freshen* and update the information.

- **Home** will bring you to the first page you see when you start the Internet. AOL users don't have this option.

Changing your Internet start page

Netscape 4.0 or greater

1. Click on EDIT from the menus.
2. Click on PREFERENCES.

3. Look for the Home Page section on the right and type the address of the page you want to start with.
4. Click on OK.

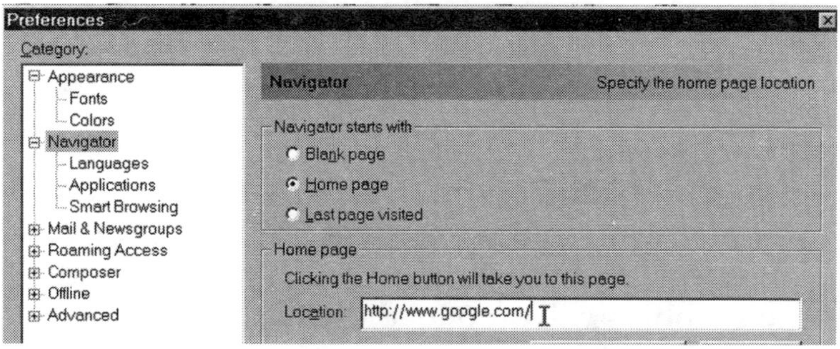

***Tip within a tip*:**
If you are currently viewing the page you want to be your start page, then follow steps 1-2 and then click on the USE CURRENT PAGE button and then OK.

Internet Explorer

1. Click on TOOLS from the menus.
2. Click on INTERNET TOOLS (or OPTIONS).
3. Look for the Home Page section on the right and type the address of the page you want to start with.
4. Click on OK.

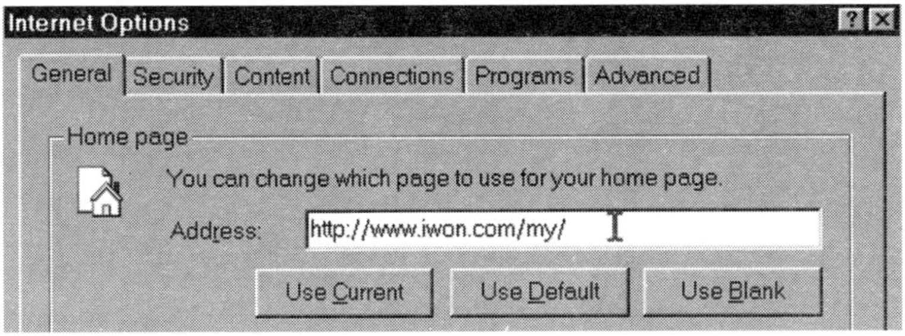

Tip within a tip:
If you are currently viewing the page you want to be your start page, then follow steps 1-2 and then click on the USE CURRENT button and then OK.

Searching the Internet with directories

One of the most frustrating tasks for any computer user is finding new information quickly on the Internet.

With more than a billion Web pages available (and more every day), the Internet reigns as the largest and most accessible information storehouse that the world has ever known.

Let's start with a method of searching that is familiar to all of us, libraries. Yahoo! and Snap.com (and others) provide Internet users a directory of the Internet that is organized just like the library.

If you were looking for a map to Australia in the library, you must first go to the reference section then the geography section and then you find the maps of international countries and look for Australia.

Internet directory services work the same way. You start at their home page and click on a general category. Use your mouse to zero in on the more specific category.

Here's how we would find a small town newspaper in Iowa using the Yahoo! directory service.

1. At the Yahoo! Web page, we will read through their topic listings and find one that says NEWS and click on it.
2. Now we see various types of news and we will look for NEWSPAPERS and click on it.
3. Here we can see that there are topics for international newspapers college newspapers and many others, click on REGIONAL.
4. Click on U.S. STATES.
5. Now you will see a list of all fifty states, find IOWA and click on it.
6. On this page, click on ALL LISTINGS.
7. Now all the available newspapers in Iowa are there to sort through.

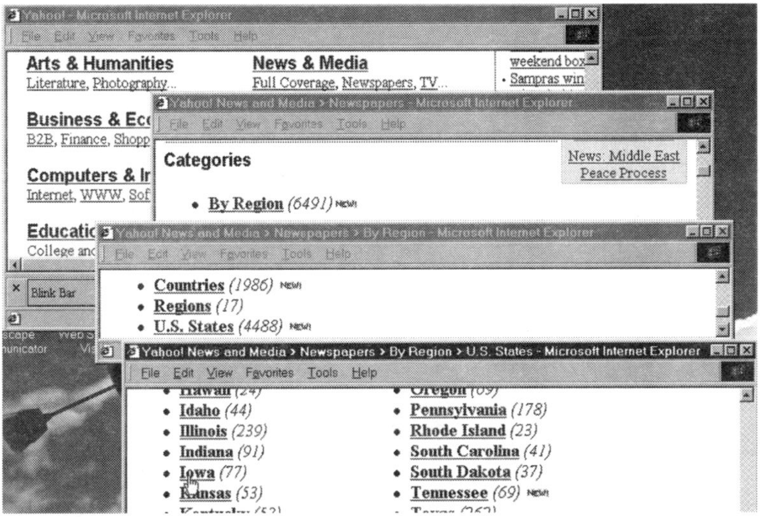

If you are new to the Internet or having a difficult time finding information, using a directory service and the above method of starting with a general search and refining it to the more specific topic, your success in searching the Internet will greatly improve.

Search engines

A search engine is a Web page that allows you to type in a question or a few keywords and have the Web page scour the Internet for Web sites that have content coinciding with your keywords or question.

The problem with the Internet and searching lies in the fact that there are many different types of search engines and no one search engine searches and indexes the Internet in the same way.

This is the reason why you can get drastically different results from two different search engines. Also, keep in mind that search engines only have the ability, currently, to index about fifteen to twenty percent of the Internet. And because they do index and search the Internet in different ways, they do not necessarily index and search the *same* fifteen percent.

***Tip within a tip*:**
If you do not find information you are looking for through one search engine, it is a must to try alternate search engines.

I use Ask Jeeves (www.ask.com) as a starting point for many of my searches for two reasons:

1. You can use plain English and ask a question as if you're asking your neighbor or friend.
2. Not only does it search its own store of information, but it also searches four to five other top search engines at the same time.

So in effect, searching this way allows you to simultaneously search up to six search engines at one time. This drastically reduces the time you spend trying to extract information from the Internet.

Simply type in a question and click on the ASK button (or press enter on your keyboard).

Here is what a page of answers looks like from Jeeves. Scroll through it and then click on the ASK button next to the answer you want to look at:

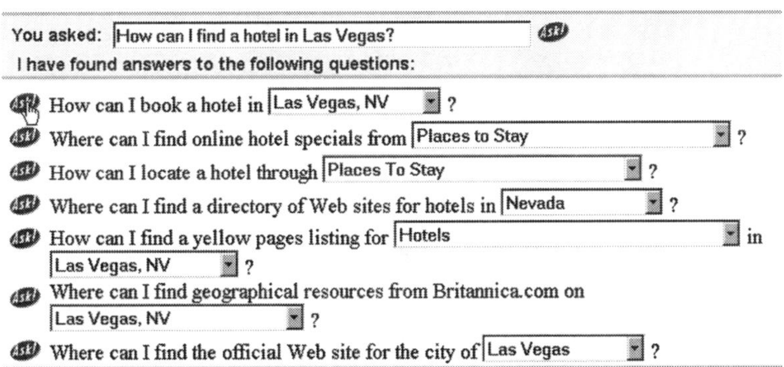

***Tip within a tip*:**
One slight irritation I have with Jeeves is that he puts up a *banner* at the top of the answer page.

To get rid of it, click on the CLOSE FRAME option from that banner.

Ask Jeeves is known as a *meta search engine* because it searches multiple search engines at the same time. Other good meta search engines are:

- www.google.com
- www.metacrawler.com
- www.search.com

Most search engines will take multiple words and search for them as a phrase. So, instead of searching for just a single word or topic, be more specific with your search.

Example:

Alta Vista Search Results

Search Term	**Number of Web pages found**
Trunks	90,000
Antiques	1.6 million
Antique trunks	160

As I mentioned, when you search for multiple words, most search sites will keep the words together as a phrase versus separate words, but to make sure you can put quotes around the words.

Web portals—your own custom newspaper

A Web portal allows you to customize the content you see on a particular Web page. Spend a few minutes to select your own custom:

- news
- sports and scores
- weather information
- entertainment
- stock quotes
- and more!

A sample can be found on the following page:

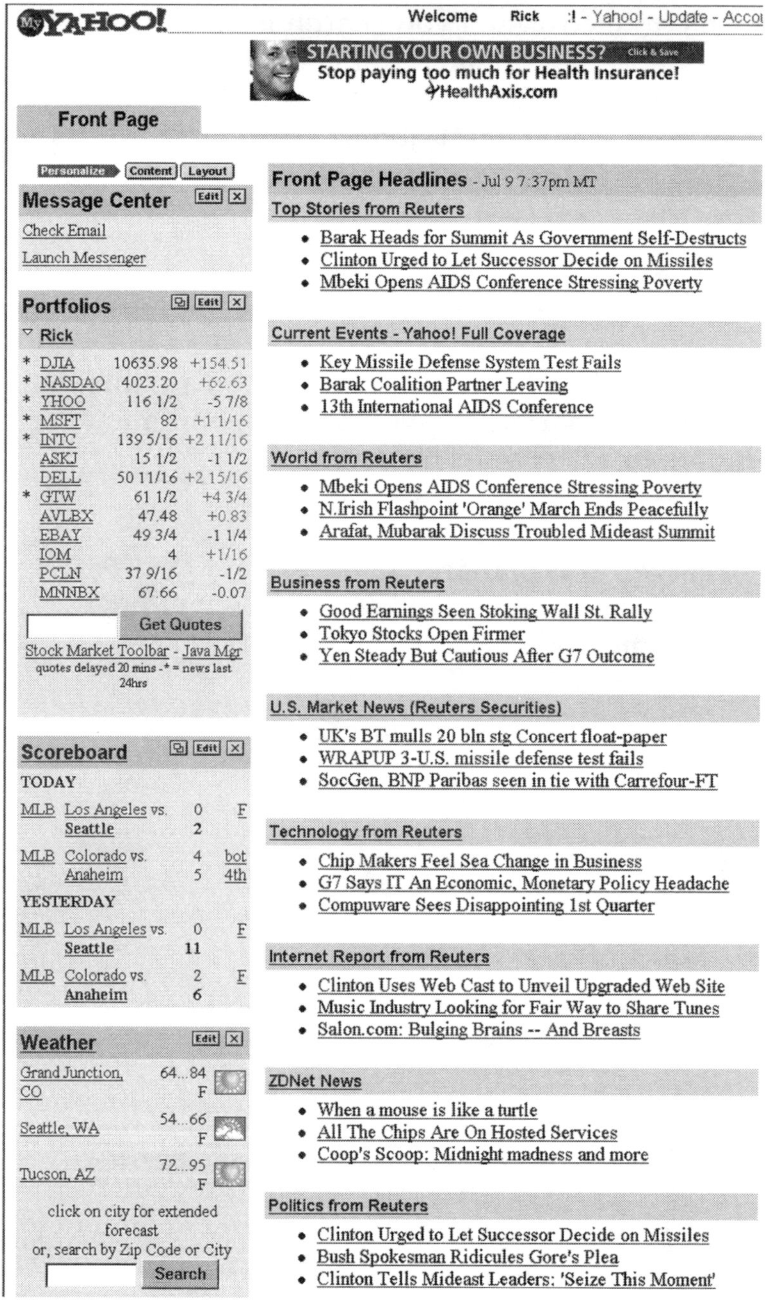
My YAHOO!
Welcome Rick :! - Yahoo! - Update - Accou
STARTING YOUR OWN BUSINESS? Click & Save
Stop paying too much for Health Insurance!
HealthAxis.com
Front Page
Personalize Content Layout
Message Center Edit
Check Email
Launch Messenger
Portfolios Edit
Rick
* DJIA 10635.98 +154.51
* NASDAQ 4023.20 +62.63
* YHOO 116 1/2 -5 7/8
* MSFT 82 +1 1/16
* INTC 139 5/16 +2 11/16
ASKJ 15 1/2 -1 1/2
DELL 50 11/16 +2 15/16
* GTW 61 1/2 +4 3/4
AVLBX 47.48 +0.83
EBAY 49 3/4 -1 1/4
IOM 4 +1/16
PCLN 37 9/16 -1/2
MNNBX 67.66 -0.07
Get Quotes
Stock Market Toolbar - Java Mgr
quotes delayed 20 mins - * = news last 24hrs
Scoreboard Edit
TODAY
MLB Los Angeles vs. Seattle 0 2 F
MLB Colorado vs. Anaheim 4 5 bot 4th
YESTERDAY
MLB Los Angeles vs. Seattle 0 11 F
MLB Colorado vs. Anaheim 2 6 F
Weather Edit
Grand Junction, CO 64...84 F
Seattle, WA 54...66 F
Tucson, AZ 72...95 F
click on city for extended forecast
or, search by Zip Code or City
Search
Front Page Headlines - Jul 9 7:37pm MT
Top Stories from Reuters
Barak Heads for Summit As Government Self-Destructs
Clinton Urged to Let Successor Decide on Missiles
Mbeki Opens AIDS Conference Stressing Poverty
Current Events - Yahoo! Full Coverage
Key Missile Defense System Test Fails
Barak Coalition Partner Leaving
13th International AIDS Conference
World from Reuters
Mbeki Opens AIDS Conference Stressing Poverty
N.Irish Flashpoint 'Orange' March Ends Peacefully
Arafat, Mubarak Discuss Troubled Mideast Summit
Business from Reuters
Good Earnings Seen Stoking Wall St. Rally
Tokyo Stocks Open Firmer
Yen Steady But Cautious After G7 Outcome
U.S. Market News (Reuters Securities)
UK's BT mulls 20 bln stg Concert float-paper
WRAPUP 3-U.S. missile defense test fails
SocGen, BNP Paribas seen in tie with Carrefour-FT
Technology from Reuters
Chip Makers Feel Sea Change in Business
G7 Says IT An Economic, Monetary Policy Headache
Compuware Sees Disappointing 1st Quarter
Internet Report from Reuters
Clinton Uses Web Cast to Unveil Upgraded Web Site
Music Industry Looking for Fair Way to Share Tunes
Salon.com: Bulging Brains -- And Breasts
ZDNet News
When a mouse is like a turtle
All The Chips Are On Hosted Services
Coop's Scoop: Midnight madness and more
Politics from Reuters
Clinton Urged to Let Successor Decide on Missiles
Bush Spokesman Ridicules Gore's Plea
Clinton Tells Mideast Leaders: 'Seize This Moment'

Good portals to look at and compare include:

- www.yahoo.com
- www.iwon.com
- www.excite.com
- www.nbci.com

Portals provide the service for free, and it makes a great Web starting point.

Organizing the web

Great, now that you can find and navigate to all types of information on the Web, how do you save it and more importantly find it again?

When you come across a Web page that you want to keep and refer to later, follow these instructions:

Netscape Bookmarks

1. As you are viewing the Web page you want to keep, click on the BOOKMARKS option from the toolbar.

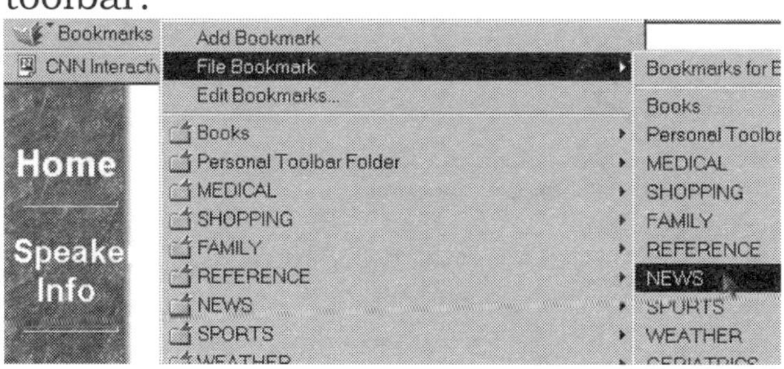

2. Click on FILE BOOKMARK.
3. Click on a category that fits the Web page.

To navigate back to the Web site you saved:

1. Click on BOOKMARKS.
2. Click on the category where you saved the bookmark.
3. Click on the Web site.

***Tip within a tip*:**
To create the categories that you see above:

1. Click on BOOKMARKS.
2. Click on EDIT BOOKMARKS.
3. Click on FILE from the menus.
4. Click on NEW FOLDER.
5. Type a name for the folder.
6. Click on OK.

Tip within a tip within a tip:
If you have already saved a lot of bookmarks, but have never created categories, you can organize by creating the categories and then dragging the saved Web pages to the appropriate category.

Internet Explorer

1. As you are viewing the Web page you want to keep, click on FAVORITES from the menus.
2. Click on ADD TO FAVORITES.

3. Click on a folder (category) where you want to store that Web page.
4. Click on OK.

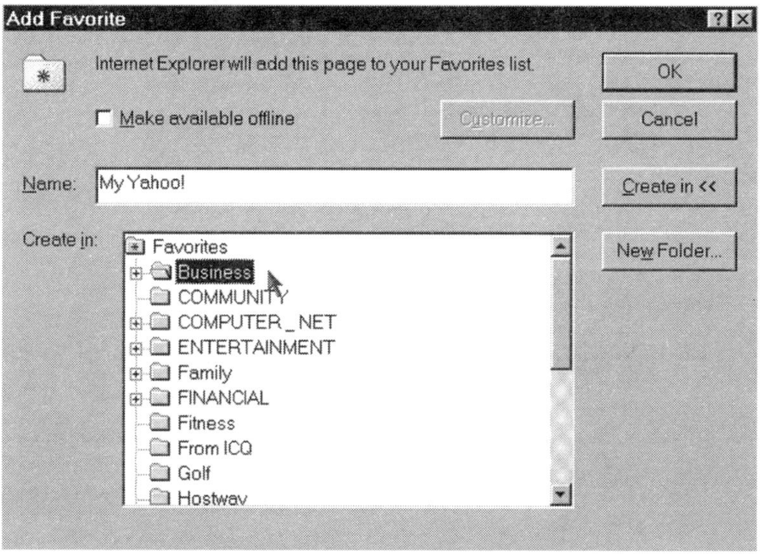

To navigate back to the Web site you saved:

1. Click on FAVORITES from the menus.
2. Click on the category where you saved the favorite.
3. Click on the Web site.

Tip within a tip:
Note that Internet Explorer lets you create your categories (folders) on the fly. If you are in need of a new category, click on the NEW FOLDER button to create it.

AOL Favorites

When you reach an AOL page or Web page that you want to add to your favorites, Click on the little heart in the upper right-hand corner of the window.

Tip within a tip:
You can organize your favorites in AOL by clicking on FAVORITES from the toolbar, then EDIT FAVORITES.

Quick access to frequently visited Web sites

Bookmarks and favorites are great for organizing and having quick access to your favorite Web pages, but what if you visit a Web site every day?

Sites like weather or stock quotes can be accessed with one click via the customized toolbars in Internet Explorer and Netscape Communicator (AOL users do not have this option).

Internet Explorer

As you are viewing the Web page you want to keep, click and drag the little icon next to the Web site address to the LINKS toolbar and release. You will then have a *button* for that particular Web site.

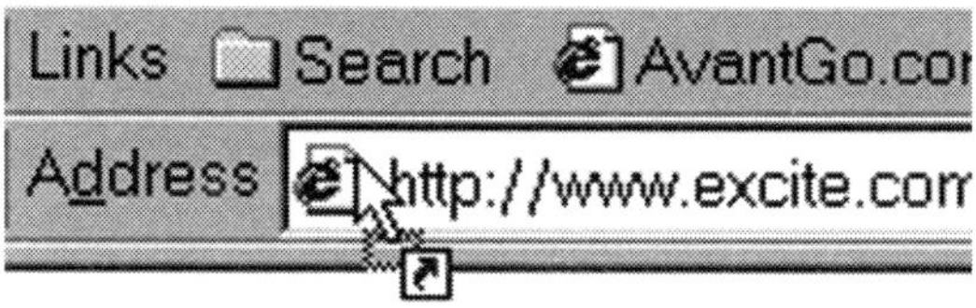

Netscape Communicator

As you are viewing the Web page you want to keep, click and drag the little BOOKMARK to the left of the Web site address to the toolbar and release. You will then have a button for that particular Web site

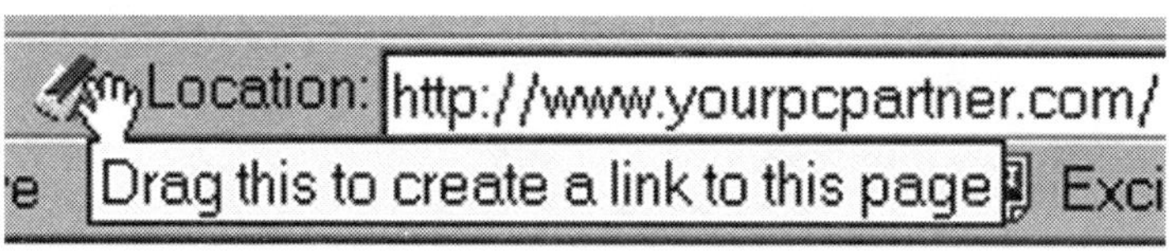

Tip within a tip:
For you "Type A" personalities, you can create a folder or category on the custom toolbars to store multiple quick access sites (see the picture of my Search category in Internet Explorer).

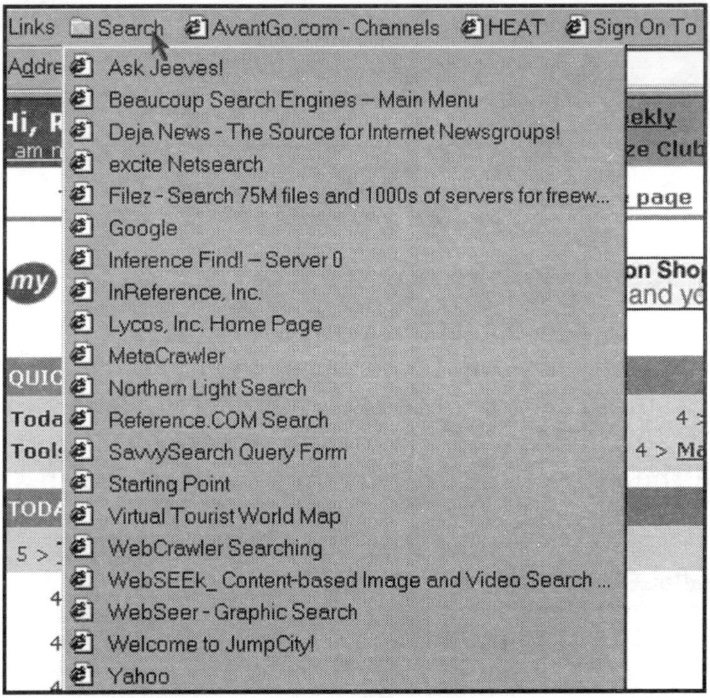

Free email

Do you have a household full of computer users and only one email address? You can each have your own personal address by signing up for free email from one of many sites on the Web including:

- www.mail.com
- www.hotmail.com
- www.yahoo.com
- www.excite.com
- www.netscape.com

Tip within a tip:
A bonus of these types of email accounts is that you can access them from any Internet enabled computer in the world!

AOL users can access their email via the Web at this address: www.aol.com

Adding an email notification sound to your email

Who believes that "You've got mail!" is not only horrible grammar, but also kind of corny?

If you are an AOL user and want to change that sound or an independent Internet user who uses Netscape, or Outlook Express, Eudora, etc. for your mail, this tip will help you add your own customized sound to your email.

The first thing you need is a sound file. You can get this one of three ways:

1. Use the stock sounds that come with Windows.
2. Download a sound from the Internet.
3. Or, my favorite, record your own sound (children, grandchildren, friend, dog, etc.).

Once you have the sound you want to try, follow these steps:

1. Click on START.
2. Click on SETTINGS.
3. Click on CONTROL PANEL.
4. Double-click on SOUNDS.
5. Scroll through the list of events and look for *New Mail Notification.* (If you are an AOL user, find your email sound under the AOL heading in this event box.)
6. Click once on NEW MAIL NOTIFICATION.

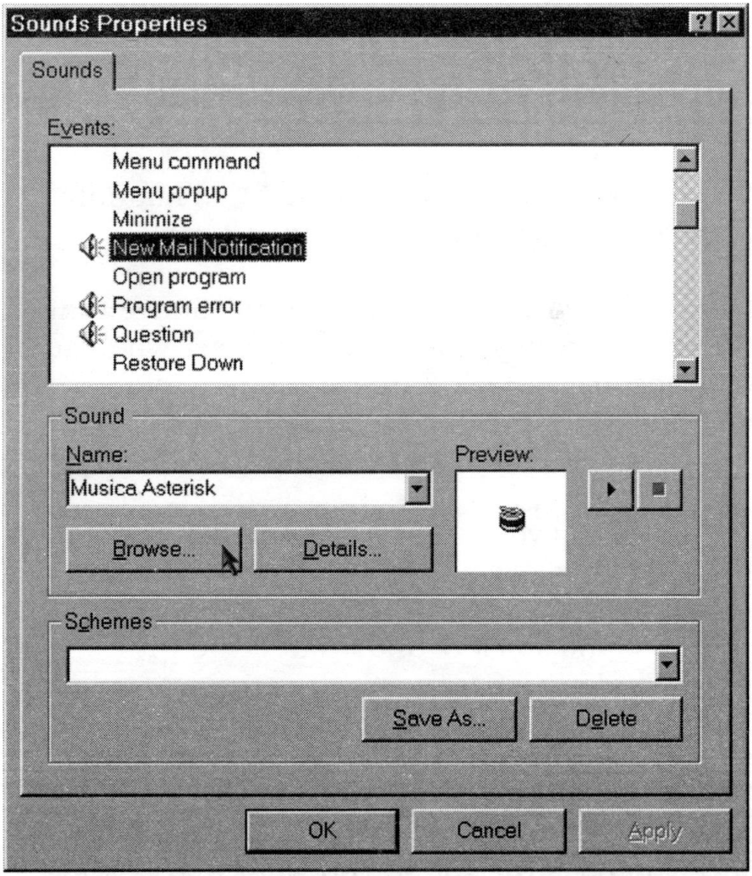

7. About halfway down the page, click on the BROWSE button underneath the Name box and navigate to where your sound file is and double-click on it.
8. Click OK.

One last point about sound and email: make sure that your individual email program is set to automatically check email and that it saves your password.

From now on you will have a nice, customized auditory signal for new email.

***Tip within a tip*:**
If you were wondering how to create your own sound, do this:

1. Click on START.
2. Click on PROGRAMS.
3. Click on ACCESSORIES.
4. Click on MULTIMEDIA (or ENTERTAINMENT on some computers).

5. Click on SOUND RECORDER.

6. Click on the RECORD button.
7. Speak into your microphone (keep it under three to four seconds).
8. Click on the STOP button when you are finished.
9. Click on FILE.
10. Click on SAVE.

Creating an email address book

Netscape Communicator

1. Click on COMMUNICATOR from the menus.
2. Click on ADDRESS BOOK.
3. Click on the NEW CARD button.

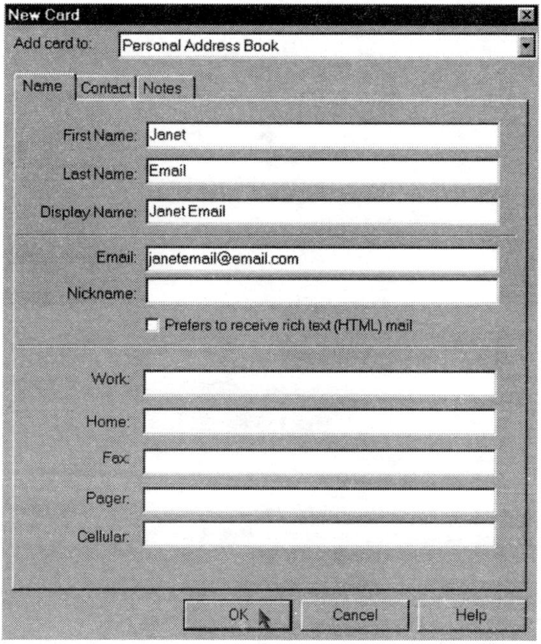

4. Fill in the form (make sure the email address is accurate).
5. Click on OK.

Tip within a tip:
With Communicator, you can add a person to your email very quickly by clicking on his/her name in a mail that you received.

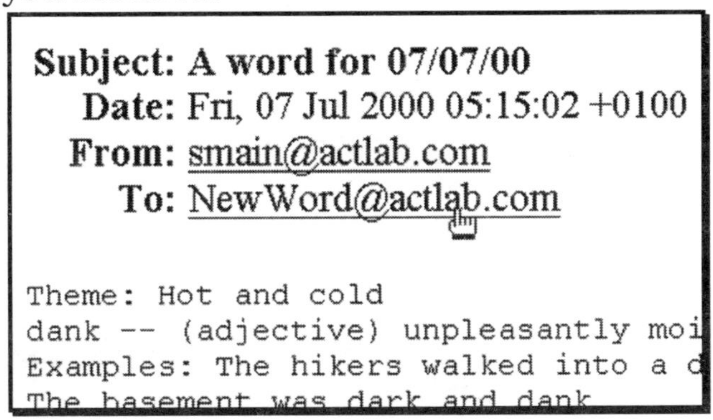

Outlook Express

1. Click on TOOLS from the menus.
2. Click on ADDRESS BOOK (or click on ADDRESS BOOK button on the toolbar).

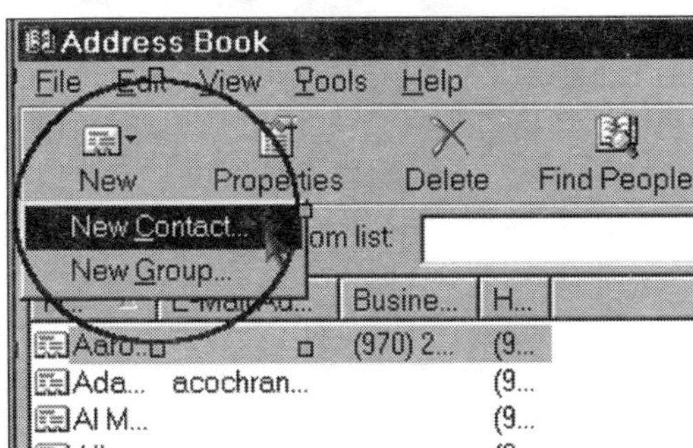

3. Click on NEW and then CONTACT from the toolbar.
4. Fill in the form (make sure the email address is accurate).
5. Click on OK.

***Tip within a tip*:**
To add a person to your address book who has sent you an email:

1. Click on TOOLS.
2. Click on ADD SENDER TO ADDRESS BOOK.

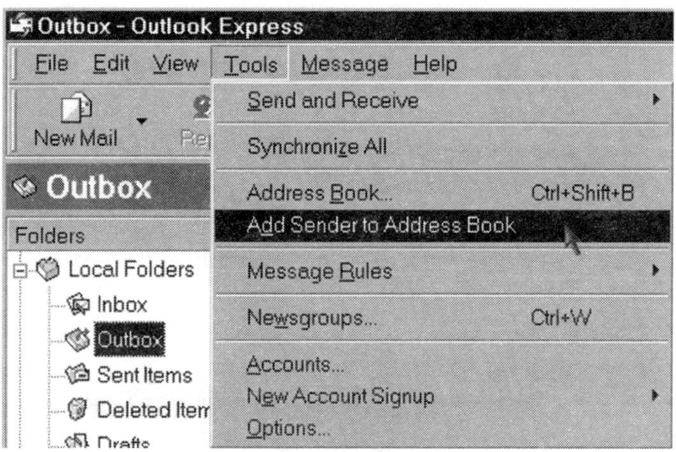

AOL

1. Click on MAIL CENTER from the menus.
2. Click on ADDRESS BOOK.

3. Click on NEW PERSON.
4. Fill in the form (make sure the email address is accurate).
5. Click OK.

Tip within a tip:
To add a person to your address book who has sent you an email:

1. Open any piece of email.
2. Highlight the email address(es) you want to add to your address book.
3. Click ADD ADDRESS.

Backup your address book

Once you have your address book built, keep it safe by creating a backup on a floppy disk.

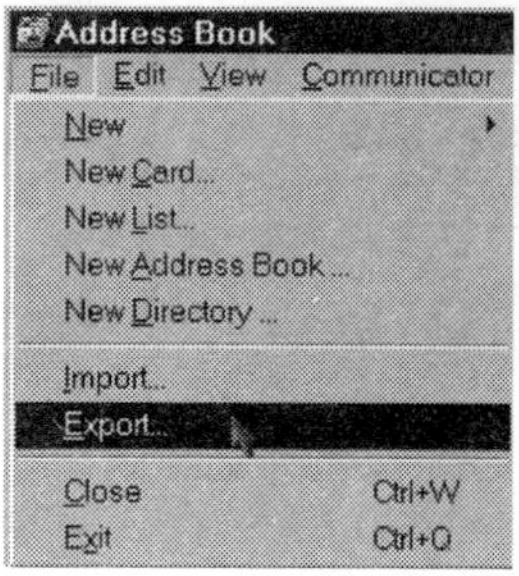

Netscape Communicator

1. Start Netscape Communicator.
2. Click on COMMUNICATOR from the menus.
3. Click on ADDRESS BOOK.
4. In the address book window, Click on FILE → EXPORT.

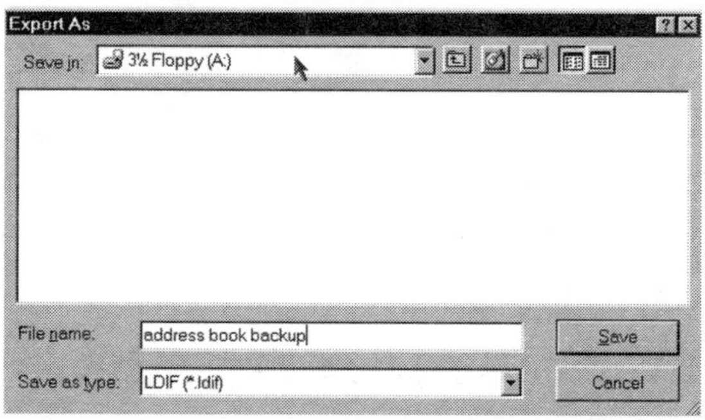

5. Click in the SAVE IN box and choose 3½″ FLOPPY (make sure there is a disk inserted into your computer).
6. Type: address book backup in the file name box.
7. Click on SAVE.

Outlook Express

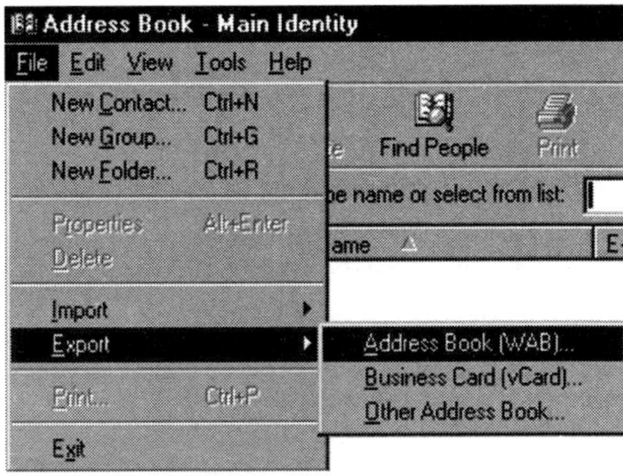

1. Start Outlook Express.
2. Click on TOOLS from the menus.
3. Click on ADDRESS BOOK.
4. In the Address Book window, click on FILE → EXPORT from the menus.

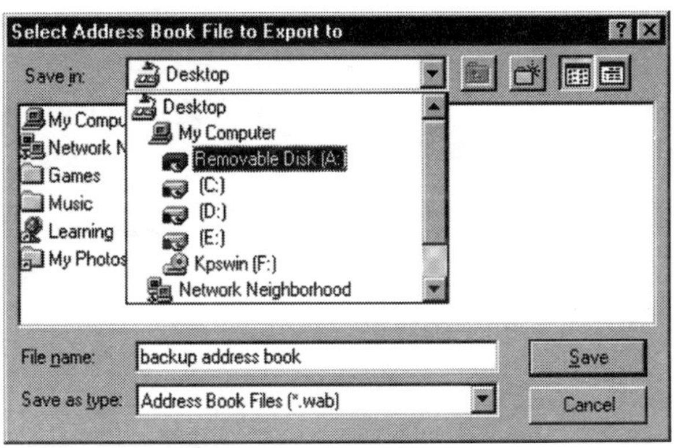

5. Click in the SAVE IN box and choose 3½″ FLOPPY (make sure there is a disk inserted into your computer).
6. Type: backup address book in the file name box.
7. Click on SAVE.

AOL

1. Click on MAIL CENTER from the menus.
2. Click on ADDRESS BOOK.
3. Click on SAVE/REPLACE.
4. Click in the SAVE IN box and choose 3½″ FLOPPY (make sure there is a disk inserted into your computer).
5. Type: backup address book in the file name box.
6. Click on SAVE.

Cleaning up headers in email before printing

Are you frustrated with email header (email addresses, dates, etc.) information and want to learn how to print email without all the headers? This technique will work no matter what email program you are using.

The only way to get rid of headers when printing is to follow this procedure:

1. Start your email session as normal
2. Keep your email open, but now click on START→PROGRAMS→ACCESSORIES→NOTEPAD.
3. This will open up the small program called Notepad (notice that you now have two buttons on the bar next to the Start button; one for your email and one for Notepad.

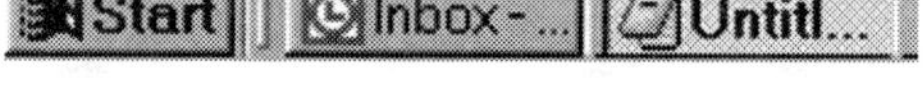

4. Click on your email program button.
5. Now select the text, with your mouse, in the email that you want to print (leaving out all the forward information).
6. Click on EDIT from the menus at the top of the screen.
7. Click on COPY.
8. Click on the NOTEPAD button at the bottom of the screen.
9. Click on the EDIT menu in Notepad.
10. Click on PASTE.

Now only the information you want remains. Print from the file menu in notepad.

***Tip within a tip*:**
To forward a message without the headers, follow the exact procedure above, but instead of pasting the information into Notepad, paste the information into a NEW email.

Cleaning up forwarded email

How do you get rid of those annoying >>>> in an email message so that you can print or pass on a clean email?
My first rule: **Do not forward**! Instead copy and paste the information you want to send on to someone else in a new email message.

Here's how to get rid of the >>>> (forward characters):

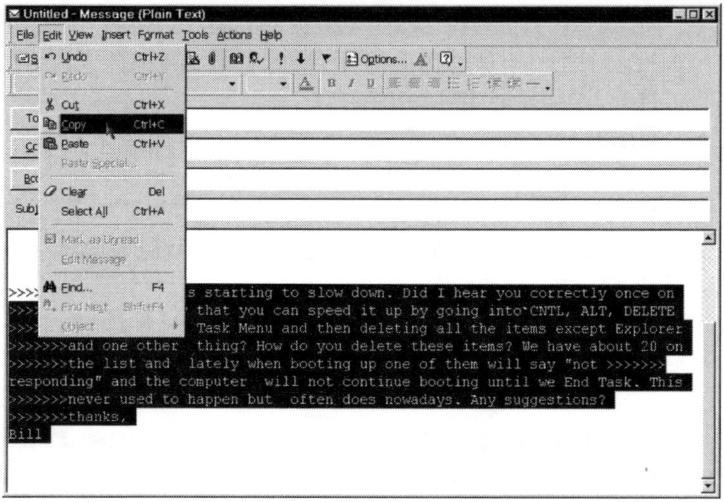

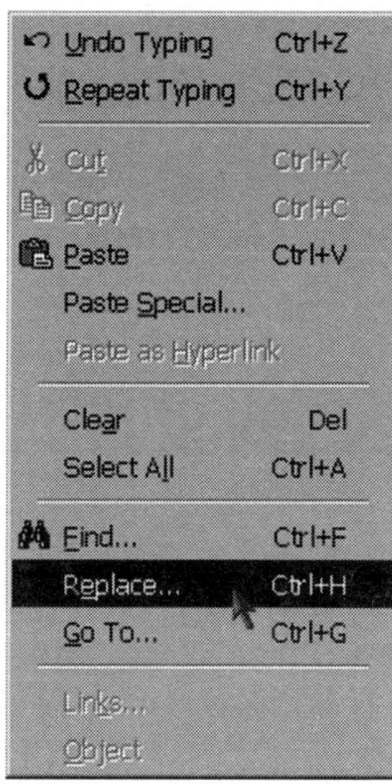

1. Highlight the text you want to send to someone else.
2. Click on EDIT from the menus.
3. Click on COPY.
4. Click on START.
5. Click on PROGRAMS.
6. Click on your favorite word processor (Word, WordPerfect, etc.).
7. Click on EDIT.
8. Click on PASTE.
9. Click on EDIT.
10. Click on REPLACE.
11. In the dialog box that pops up, type the offending character ONE time in the Find

What box (usually it's the angle bracket character >).

12. Leave the Replace with box empty.
13. Click on REPLACE ALL.
14. Click OK.

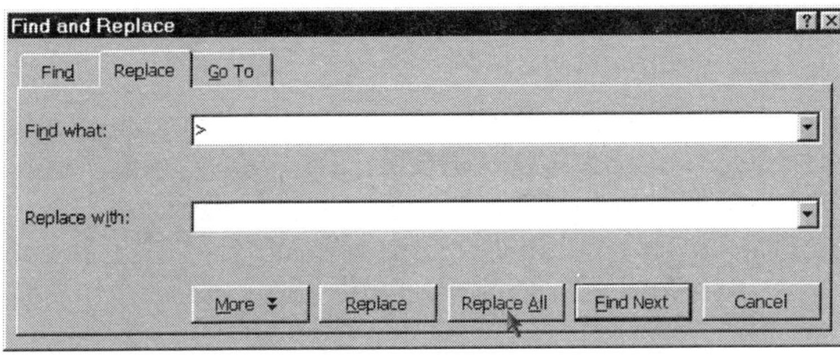

15. Click CLOSE.
16. Instant bliss! All the >>> are gone.

Now you have to get this cleaned up text back to your email:

17. Click on EDIT from the menus.
18. Click on SELECT ALL.
19. Click on EDIT again.
20. Click on COPY.
21. Close your word processor and return to your email program (don't save the document when prompted).
22. Start a new email message, address it and add a subject as normal.
23. When the cursor is in the body of your message, click on EDIT from the menus.
24. Click on PASTE.

Don't be intimidated by the number of steps to accomplish this cleanup maneuver. It only takes a moment or two to complete and the result is exactly what you wanted.

Sending email blindly

If you plan on sending an email to more than a few people, use the BCC or *blind carbon copy* function. This allows you to still send the email to all the people on your list, but the recipients will not see any of the people to whom the mail was addressed.

Netscape Communicator

Click on the little TO button and the BCC will be a choice (If you have a version less than 4.5, you will have to have at least one person in the *to* category).

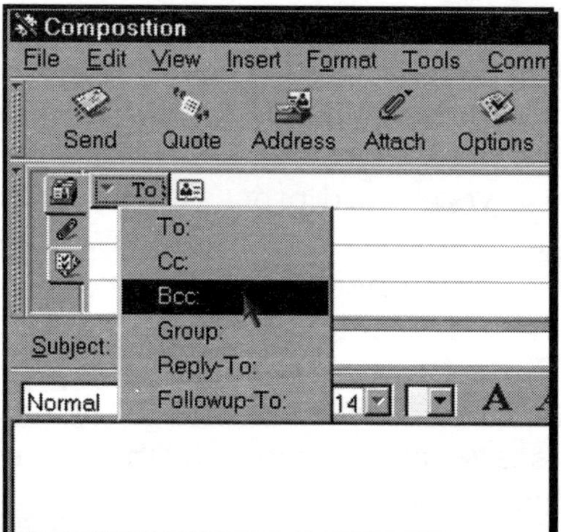

OR you can click on the BCC button from your address book when you add names from the address book.

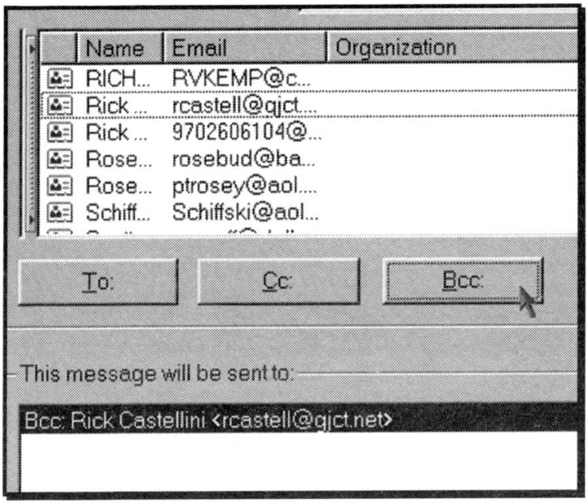

Outlook or Outlook Express

You will need to use the address book to select your recipients, but instead of clicking on the TO button, use the BCC button.

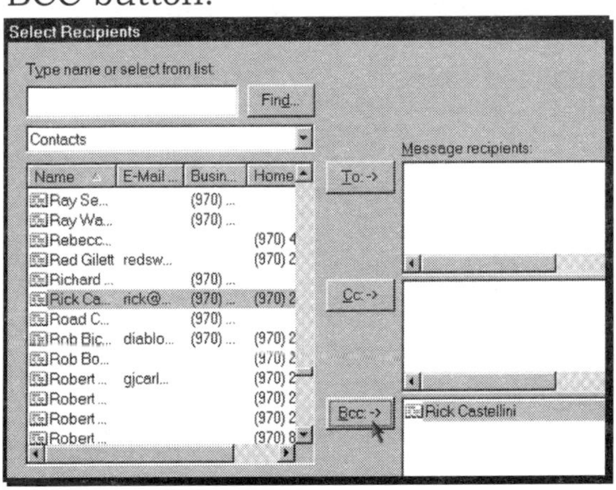

AOL

Similar to the Outlook users, you can access the BCC function from your address book.

Sending attachments

Attachments are the pictures, documents, spreadsheets and other files that *ride* along with an email. Here's how to send attachments with your email:

Outlook Express

Start a new email as normal complete with address, subject and any text you want in the body, then:

1. Click on ATTACH from the toolbar (looks like a paperclip).
2. Navigate to where you the file you want to attach is stored.
3. Click on the file to attach and then on the ATTACH button in the lower right hand corner.
4. Send as normal.

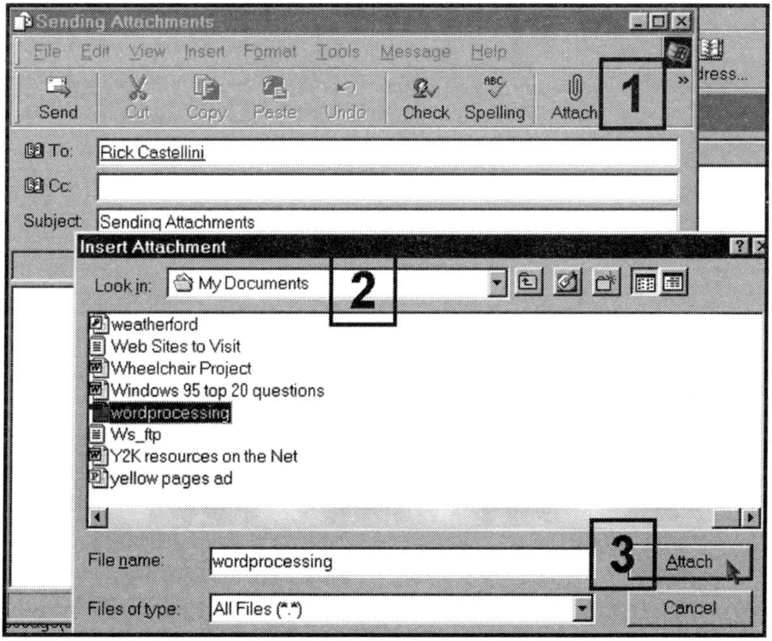

Netscape Communicator

Start a new email as normal complete with address, subject and any text you want in the body, then:

1. Click on ATTACH → FILE from the toolbar.
2. Navigate to the file you want to attach.
3. Click on the file to attach, and then click on the OPEN button.
4. Send as normal.

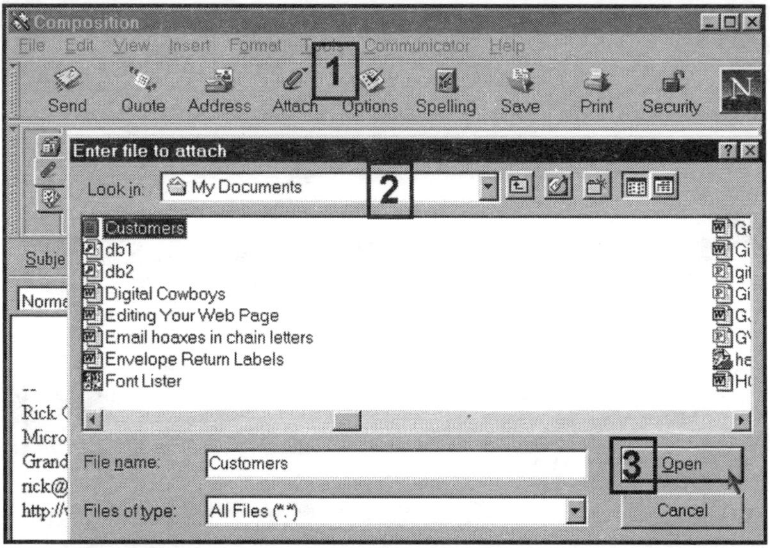

AOL Email

Start a new email as normal complete with address, subject and any text you want in the body, then:

1. Click on the ATTACHMENTS button in the lower left-hand corner of the email message.
2. Click on ATTACH again in the next window and navigate to the file you want to send and double-click on it.
3. The file should now appear in the Attachment Window.
4. Click OK to return back to your email.
5. Send as normal.

Tip within a tip:
You can attach multiple files to the same email by just following steps 1-3 for your respective email as many times as necessary.

IMPORTANT NOTE: Try not to attach files larger than about 600 kilobytes per email. Files larger than this transfer slowly across phone lines.

Attaching photos to email

Attaching photos mimics the above techniques exactly. However, learning to format your photos correctly for email will make sending them much easier for you and the recipient. Keep these rules in mind:

- Always save photos in JPEG format for email.
- Depending on the photo-editing program you use the wording may be different, but avoid sending a photo larger than 550 pixels wide.
- Some of the more popular photo editing programs allow you to "save picture for email or Web." Use this feature to automate and optimize the process.
- Crop photos so that unnecessary portions of the picture are discarded.
- Anything less than 250 kilobytes is a good file size for a photo to be sent via email.

What is a mime file?

America Online software automatically encodes some email attachments using an encoding called MIME.

If your AOL email reader can't handle an attachment, it automatically gets translated into a file with an .mme extension or .mim extension. You will notice when this happens by the fact you can't open an attachment or the attachment looks like a bunch of indecipherable letters when it does open.

You can use a program called WinZip to decode these files back to their original state (usually pictures).

Just find the file in your Windows Explorer (it is usually located in your AOL folder then the Download subfolder) and double-click it.

If you do not have the WinZip program, you can download it from www.winzip.com

Download files from the Internet

You can find many types of small programs on the Web that accomplish specific tasks. These programs are called shareware (you can try the program for free, but the programmer asks for a small registration fee) or freeware (there is no charge to use the software).

The most popular sites for searching for and downloading shareware and freeware are:

- www.hotfiles.com
- www.shareware.com
- www.tucows.com

Once you find a file or program you would like to view or download, how do you get it to your computer? Follow these steps to get the program safely and successfully to your computer:

1. Click once on the file's name (some Web sites will have a download button).

2. You will be asked where to save the file before the download initiates. Pay special attention to the SAVE IN box at the top of the save screen so that you know where your file is going.

Tip within a tip:
I suggest that you download all files to the Desktop so they are easy to find.

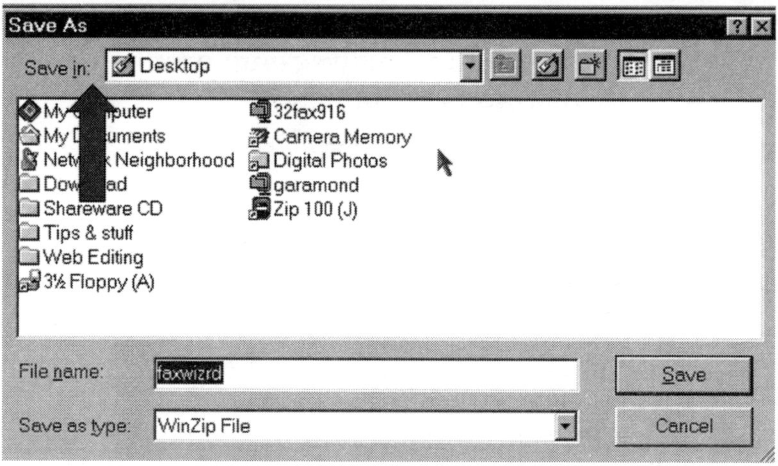

3. Click on the SAVE button and in a few seconds your download will start and you will see a progress meter showing how much of the download has completed.

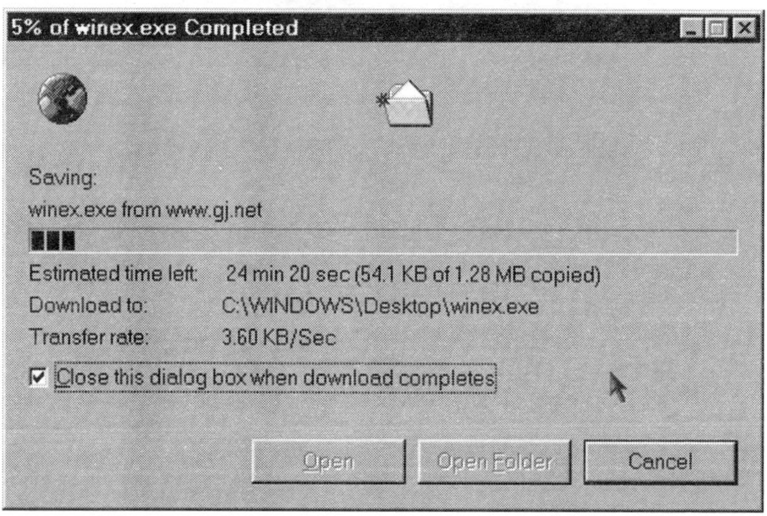

***Tip within a tip*:**
Remember that you can click back to the Web and continue surfing, writing email or doing other activities at the same time you are downloading. You do have to stay connected to your provider for the download to continue.

Also, it is possible to download more than one file at a time.

Install shareware

Once you have downloaded shareware, you now need to install it so that you can try it out.

Many shareware programs are in a compressed format called a zip file. If this is the case, then you will need a "decompression" utility such as WinZip (www.winzip.com) to get to the programs installation files.

Double-click on the file you downloaded and one of two things will happen:

1. WinZip will start and show you the files inside the *compressed package*. Look for a setup or install file and double-click on it to start the installation process.

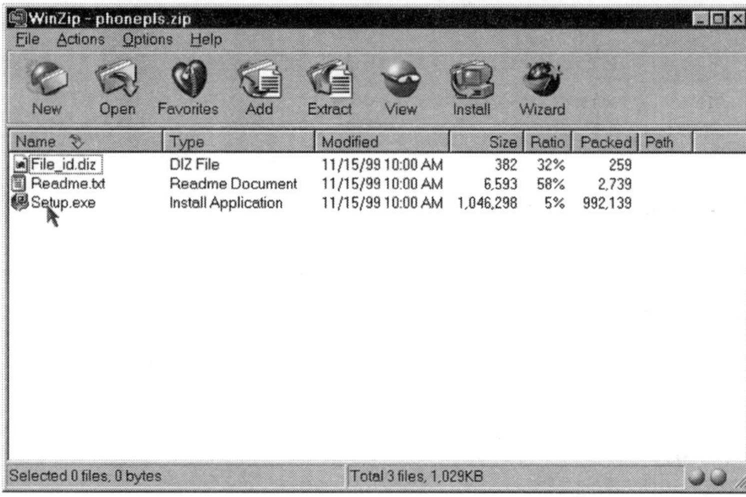

OR

2. You may have downloaded what is known as a *self-executing file*. They will generally look like this icon OR may have the icon that the product represents. Either way, simply double-click on the icon and follow the on-screen instructions.

junoinst

Making the most of dialup Internet connections

This tip teaches you how to get around the Internet faster, even with a dialup (phone) connection.

For example, when you use a search engine, it returns many different answers for you to sift through. The common way to sift through these is to click on one of the answers, examine it and then hit the back button on the browser to return to the list.

A quicker way to find what you are looking for is to:

1. Right click on a link from the answer list.
2. Click on the OPEN IN NEW WINDOW option.

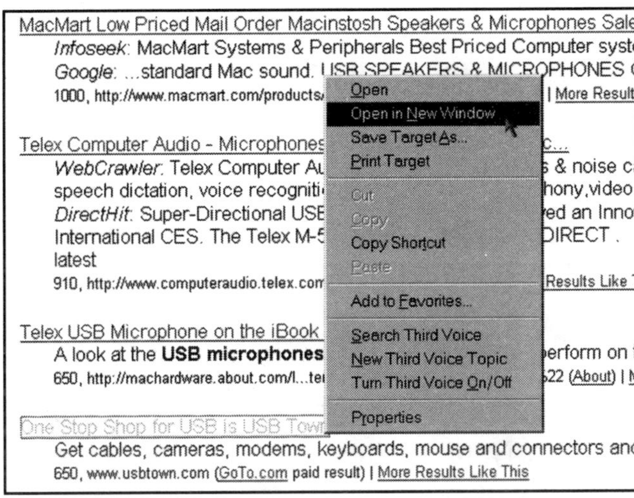

This starts a brand-new window for you to load the page. So, instead of waiting for it to download, immediately push Alt+Tab on your keyboard OR click on the alternate browser button on your taskbar to return to the list of answers.
Repeat this process as much as five times to open up Web pages simultaneously.

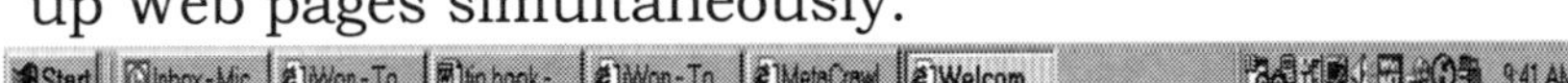

Using this technique allows you to return to the list of results while the pages you selected load in the background.

Another situation where you might want multiple browser windows is when you arrive at a page that you want to keep open, but you also want to open another page at the same time. To do this, push CONTROL+N on your keyboard to open another window.

This technique takes a little time to get comfortable with, but once you get it, you will be a happier (and faster) Web user.

Online greetings

What is an online greeting? An online (or electronic) greeting is a customizable, animated Web page or graphic that you can send to anyone with access to the Internet. Note: some email only services (such as Juno basic service) cannot receive this type of greetings.

The greetings are fun to send and receive and relatively easy to create. When you arrive at any of the greeting sites, the only information you need is the email address of the person you whom you wish to send the greeting.

Blue Mountain Arts (www.bluemountain.com) remains the most famous and frequently visited online greeting site. Blue Mountain Arts offers an enormous selection of free greetings and topics. The site loads fairly quickly and is easy to navigate.

Use your favorite search engine to search for *online greetings* and you will get a plethora of other sites. Here are some of them (not all are free):

- Greeting-Cards.com (www.greeting-cards.com)
- Cardmaster (www.cardmaster.com)
- Active Grams (www.activegrams.com)
- Yahoo! Greetings (greetings.yahoo.com)
- Hallmark (www.hallmark.com)
- American Greetings (www.americangreetings.com)

Free long-distance calls

Would you like to make free long distance calls to anyone in the country? Then give Dialpad a try.

Dialpad is a Web site that allows you to place long distance calls to anyone in the country through your Web connection!

You must have a sound card, speakers and a microphone, but you are actually calling the other party's telephone so they don't even have to own a computer!

Give it a spin at: www.dialpad.com

The quality ranges from very good to poor, but what do you expect for free? It is fun to try and use on occasion.

Other options for trying Internet phone calls are:
➲ www.firetalk.com
➲ www.web2phone.com

Tired of looking at clouds?

This tip provides instructions for adding new wallpaper to your desktop as you browse around the Internet (this tip works with Netscape, Internet Explorer, and AOL):

1. Right click on any image on any Web page.
2. Click on SAVE IMAGE AS WALLPAPER or SET AS WALLPAPER.

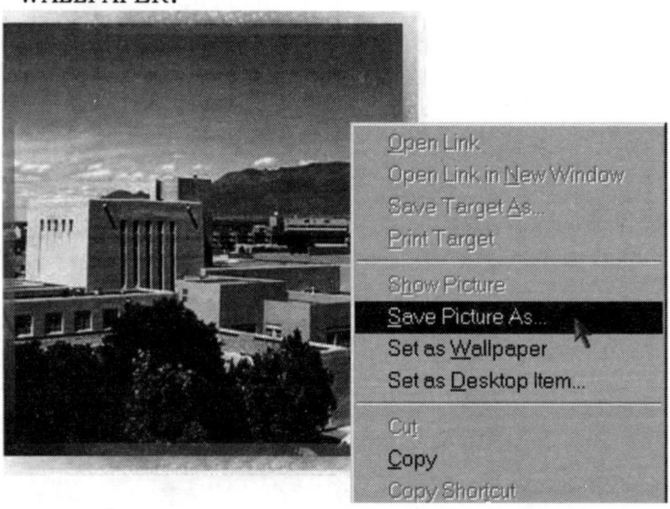

3. The image you performed this procedure on is now your desktop wallpaper.

Sorting the mail

Wouldn't it be nice if you could sort your email by the date it was received or by the name of the sender?

If you use Microsoft Outlook Express or any Netscape email program, you can quickly sort all your mail.

1. To sort the mail, click ONE time on the desired heading of your email list.
2. For example, to sort your messages chronologically, click once on the date (RECEIVED) heading to sort from oldest to newest.

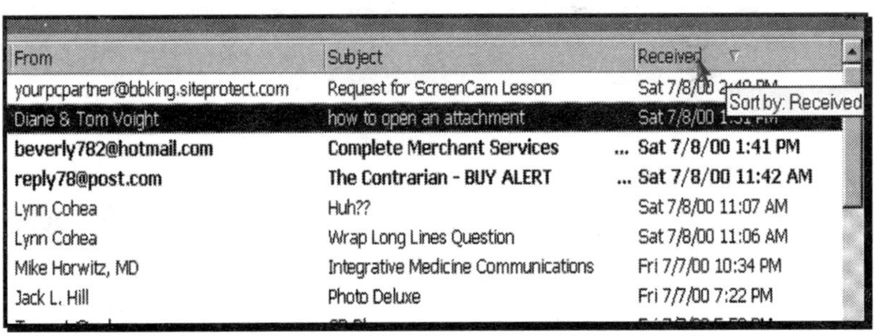

3. Click again to sort from newest to oldest.
4. To sort your mail by the sender, simply click on the FROM heading at the top of the list.

5. To sort your mail by the subject, click on the SUBJECT heading at the top of the list.

Simple, clean and useful . . . give it a try.

Fill in forms quickly

Are you tired of filling out forms using your keyboard and mouse? Try these tips to keep your hands on the keyboard and fill out those forms quicker!

➲ To quickly move from field-to-field while filling out a form, use the TAB key on your keyboard.

For example, after you fill in your name, to move the cursor from the name field to the address field, simply push the TAB key on your keyboard.

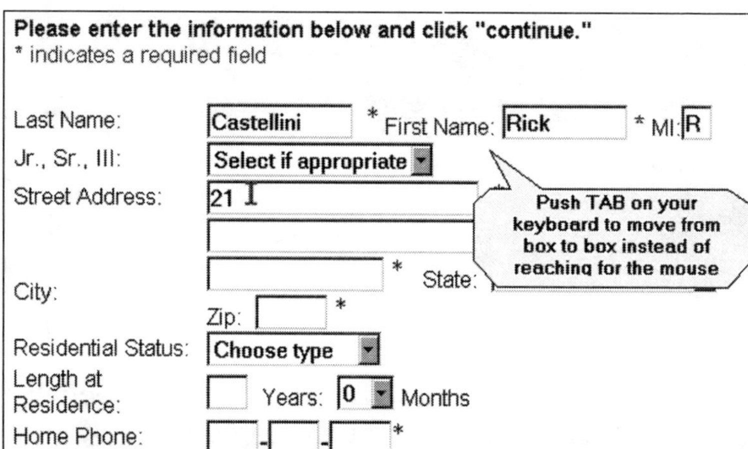

OK, so you've tabbed from Name to Address to City and now you are in the State field that has one of those drop down lists to choose the proper answer.

Normally, we reach for the mouse, click on the field, then scroll through the list and click on the proper state.

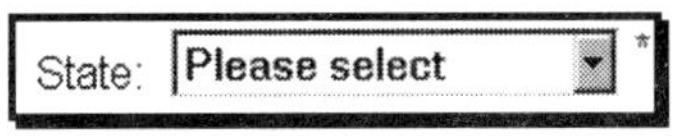

My friend Ken showed me a method of filling out these drop down boxes without using the mouse. Instead of choosing the state with the mouse, push the first letter of the state you live in and magically the list returns the first state with that letter.

So, for Colorado, when you push "C" on the keyboard, the list returns "California." Never fear, just push "C" again on the keyboard and "Colorado" pops up.

If you happen to live in Connecticut, just push "C" again. Boom! You're done with that field, push TAB on your keyboard again and carry on your merry, keyboard form filling way!

What about check boxes or radio buttons? Use the spacebar on your keyboard to toggle them on or off!

Practice this tip, amaze your friends, and save time while doing it!

Searching through the email

Many computer users know how to search the Internet for information, but did you know you could search through your email similarly? If you receive or save a lot of mail, then this tip will save you an enormous amount of time and frustration.

Look for the "Search" function in Netscape and the "Find" function in Outlook or Outlook Express. Using these tools, you can quickly search through hundreds of messages to find a specific sender, content of the message, etc.

Here's an example:

You are frantically looking for a message that was sent to you about a recipe that you would like to print. However, you can't remember who or when it was sent. You do remember that it had chocolate chips as one of the ingredients.

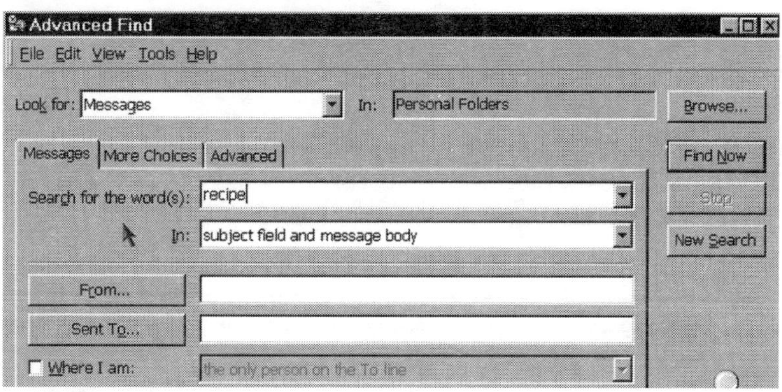

Use the find or search function for your email and search for the word “recipe” or "chocolate." In seconds, your computer will show you only those messages that contain the word chocolate.

Practice this tip a few times and you will find it an irreplaceable tool.

Keep an eye on the kids

One common question I get from parents is how to keep kids safe while using the Internet. There are many third-party programs available to filter Internet content including:

- Cyber Patrol at www.learningco.com
- Net Nanny at www.netnanny.com
- Cyber Snoop at www.pearlsw.com
- Surf Watch at www.surfwatch.com

However, if you use Internet Explorer, then you have a great tool already built into the browser itself. Here's how to use it:

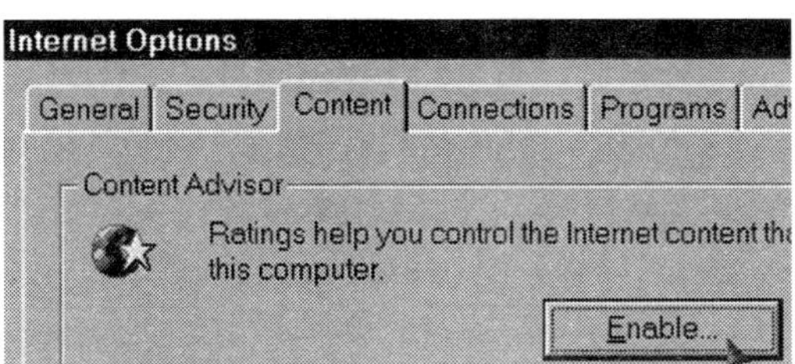

1. Click on START.
2. Click on SETTINGS.
3. Click on CONTROL PANEL.
4. Double-click on INTERNET OPTIONS (or Internet).
5. Click on the CONTENT tab.

6. Click on the ENABLE button next to the Content Advisor.
7. Use the tools provided to restrict access to Web sites that you approve (make sure that you remember and protect the password you set for this feature).

Saving a graphic or image from the Web*

This tip demonstrates how to save a graphic or photo from the Internet that you can use in a greeting card or some other print publication or for your own Web site.

1. Right click on the image or photo you want to save.
2. Click on SAVE IMAGE AS or SAVE PICTURE AS.
3. Note where you are saving the image on your system (look in the *Save In* box of the dialog box that pops up).
4. Note the name of the file (change it if you prefer).
5. Click on SAVE.
6. Now you can use your favorite program's INSERT PICTURE command to use the graphic.

*Please be aware of any copyright restrictions that some graphics may have. These can be found on the Web page where the graphic resides.

Practical Miscellaneous Tips

Selecting text on the Web or with your word processor

- Double-click on a word to select it.
- Click and drag in the margin of your word processor to select entire lines of text.
- If you have text that you need to select that spans multiple pages:
    1. Click once where you want to start selecting.
    2. Scroll down to the end of the text you want to select.
    3. Hold the SHIFT key down and click your mouse after the last word you want to select.
    4. All the text between the two points is highlighted.

Fax from your computer

One handy tool that is underutilized with our computers is the fax. Yes, you have the ability to send and receive faxes via your computer if you have a modem.

With a scanner, your computer can be as functional as a stand-alone fax machine. Without a scanner, you can send anything you create on your computer via fax and receive any faxes.

Faxing with your computer is accomplished via fax software.

If you use Windows 95, you already have Microsoft Fax installed. If you use Windows 98, the Microsoft Fax is not installed by default, but you can add it by:

1. Insert your Windows 98 CD.
2. If the auto-start screen pops up, click on the BROWSE option.
3. If your CD did not auto-start, then double-click on MY COMPUTER then double-click on your CD-ROM drive icon.
4. Double-click on the TOOLS folder
5. Double-click on the OLD WIN95 folder.
6. Double-click on the MESSAGE folder.
7. Double-click on the US folder.
8. Double-click on the AWFAX icon to install Microsoft Fax.

Tip within a tip.
You can also download numerous fax shareware programs from your favorite download site or buy commercial software such as *WinFax Pro.*

Once you have your software installed, faxing is as easy as printing.

1. Create your fax document in any Windows program.
2. Click on FILE.
3. Click on PRINT (yes, print).
4. Choose your fax program from the NAME OF PRINTER box at the top of this dialog box.
5. Click on OK.
6. Your fax software will pop up and prompt you for the recipient's name and fax number and you are on your way.

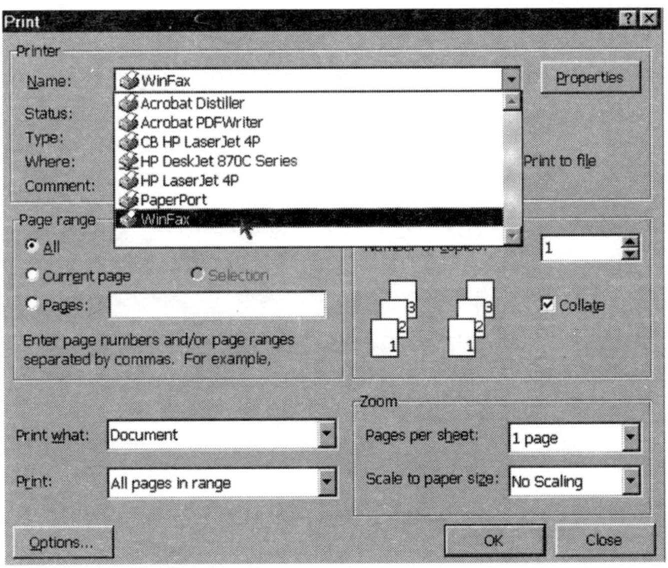

Receiving faxes is a simple matter of following the on-screen instructions provided by your particular software.

***Tip within a tip*.**
Another convenient method of receiving faxes is via email. Efax.com and jfax.com are two of many sites that offer free reception of faxes right to your email box.

Word processing

Most of us learned how to type letters and documents using a typewriter.

Word processing reigns as the new king of document creation and most typewriters are relegated to attics, back rooms and antique shops.

However, many computer users use their word processors (MS Word, Word Perfect, etc.) like a typewriter and this defeats the purpose of using the computer.

The first rule to remember when using a word processor is to:

Forget your typewriting rules.

When we sat down to our typewriters to create a document (whether a simple letter to a friend or a 500-page novel), we had to have a clear picture in our head of what the document should look like. Otherwise, crumpled typing paper littered our floors!

With word processing, the *most efficient* way to create a document is to enter all of your information first. *Then* go back and edit/change the look of your document. I have coined the phrase:

Type first. Edit last.

Editing means changing text (such as font size, bold, underline, etc.). After you have entered all of your text, you can go back and doctor up your document to make it look the way you want.

If you try to use these tools as you are typing in the text, you will become increasingly frustrated (and waste a lot of time).

Type first, edit last . . . learn it and live it when creating documents and you and your computer will be much happier companions.

Get home and back quickly!

No, the Internet has not found a way to "beam" us hither and yonder . . . yet!

I'm referring to navigating around your word processing, email or other text-related documents quickly.

Don't underestimate the power of the keyboard as you create your written masterpieces. Moving quickly from one part of your document to another saves loads of time and the keyboard can help. Try these keyboard shortcuts:

- ➲ **Home** — pressing this key will move your cursor to the beginning of a line.
- ➲ **Ctrl+Home** — moves the cursor to the beginning of a document.
- ➲ **End** — moves the cursor to the end of a line.
- ➲ **Ctrl+End** — moves the cursor to the end of a document.
- ➲ **Arrow keys** — moves your cursor around quickly in smaller but precise increments.

What is a zip file?

One question that creeps up time and time again in my weekly travels is the concept of a compressed or *zipped* file. When downloading information from the Internet, very often the file arrives in this compressed format.

Computer users use compression programs to save disk space and increase download speed. The standard compression method in the PC world is *zipping* files. WinZip has become the *de facto* standard for managing these compressed files.

As the term indicates, WinZip (and like programs) uses a complex algorithm to compress files to as little as four percent of their original size. Again, this saves both space and download time on the Internet.

If you download a file that is in the zip format and you have a program such as WinZip on your computer, simple double-clicking on the downloaded file will invoke the WinZip program. The program then asks you to choose a destination folder where you want the decompressed, usable file to reside. It then decompresses the file and stores it where you indicated so that you can view or use the file.

If you frequently share files over the Internet or archive large or numerous files, then downloading and using a program such as WinZip will benefit you greatly.

You can also use WinZip to compress and backup files on your computer.

Use online help

Every commercial (and many shareware) program contain a section of information designed to help you through questions. I hear the phrase "the help doesn't help," but read on to learn how to get the most out of help.

Microsoft Office 97/2000 Help

Microsoft adopted a *natural text* help feature (the infamous animated paperclip, *Clippie*) with the release of Office 97 in 1997. This type of help is designed to allow a user to ask a question as they would to another person and the computer decodes the question and comes up with an answer. Here's how to use that feature:

1. Click on HELP from the menus.
2. Click on MICROSOFT WORD HELP (or Excel, Outlook, etc.).
3. Click on your HELPER, usually the paperclip (*Rocky* the dog is pictured).
4. Type in a question.
5. Click on SEARCH (see illustration on the following page).

6. Fairly quickly, you will see a list of answers.
7. Click on the answer that best applies to your question.

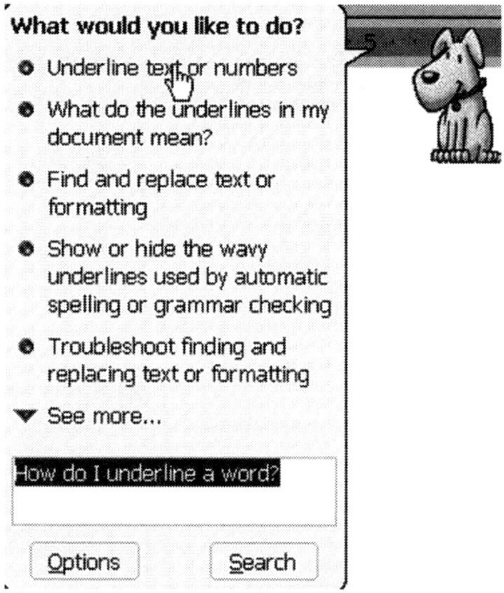

8. You should then get a fairly concise step-by-step answer.

Tip within a tip:
To change your Office helper (you will need your Office Installation CD):

1. Right click on the current helper.
2. Click on OPTIONS.
3. Click on GALLERY.
4. Click on NEXT or BACK to see your options.
5. Click on OK.

Tip within a tip within a tip:
To permanently disable the "Office helper":

1. Right click on the current helper.
2. Click on OPTIONS.
3. Uncheck the USE THE OFFICE ASSISTANT option.

Many of the other office suite products have adopted similar methods of help.

Using traditional help screens

When you click on HELP and then HELP TOPICS from most Window programs, you see this type of screen:

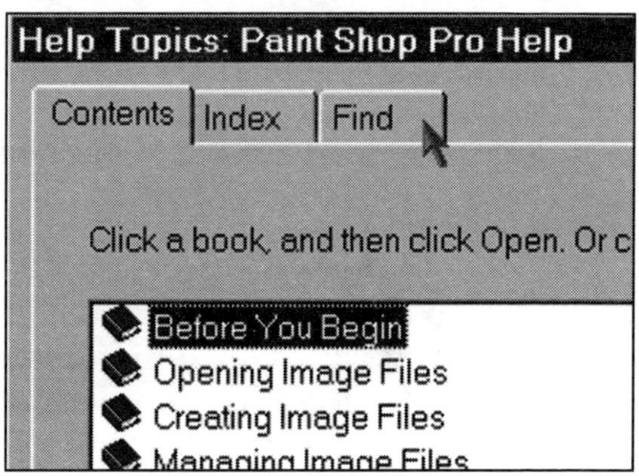

Don't bother trying to look at the Contents section. It is usually time consuming and frustrating.

The Index section is better, but can be fruitless as well.

The quickest way to find what you are looking for is to:

➲ Click on the FIND tab in the help menu.

If it is the first time you have used the help function in this particular program, you will see the following screen (see illustration on the following page):

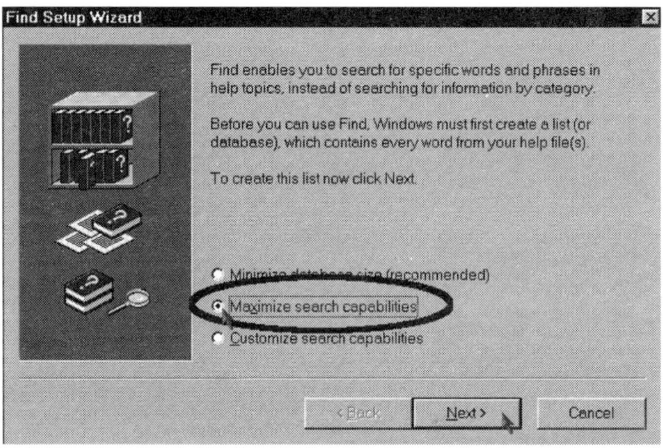

Click on the MAXIMIZE SEARCH CAPABILITIES option and then click on NEXT. Click on FINISH on the next screen, then you will see this screen:

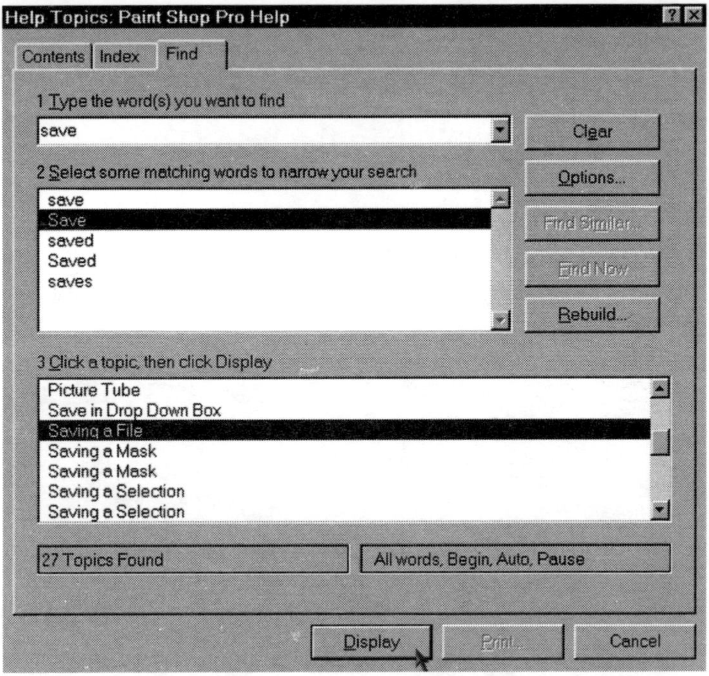

1. Type a keyword in the first box.
2. Select a word or phrase in the second box that matches what you are looking for.
3. Double-click on a topic in the third box to view the answer.

These techniques should help you get more out of your program's help features.

Expert help

If you have Internet access, I have found that using one of the volunteer "expert" sites to be a gold mine of information. The way the services work is that you visit the Web site, find the topic your question is about, find an "expert" and email him/her with your question.

It is not instant help, but often you receive an answer within hours of writing your initial email. Topics range from computers to vacation advice and everything inbetween.

Here are the top expert sites:

- www.allexperts.com
- www.askme.com
- www.expertcity.com
- www.webhelp.com

Tip within a tip:
I like to send my question to more than one expert to better my chances of getting a quick answer. Also, when the answers return, I can compare responses from the different experts.

Avoid the upgrade circle

One rut that is easy to fall into with computers is the "upgrade circle." It seems like upgrade offers for your software arrive almost weekly. And the newest high-powered computer you see in the magazine centerfold makes you drool.

I'm here to tell you: Stop, evaluate and then decide. If your current computer and software accomplishes all of your needs without a hitch, do not upgrade.

Many a computer user gets by just fine with an early Pentium computer, 32 megabytes of RAM, a 2-gigabyte or less hard drive, 28.8 modem, Windows 95 and a copy of Microsoft Works.

This list provides a few reasons why you might *need* to upgrade:

- Your hard drive storage is inadequate.
- You are a graphic artist or CAD worker and need to stay fast for productivity.
- Your computer does not meet the minimum requirements needed for a software that you need to run.

Tip within a tip:
Often, an older computer can get a great boost in performance by installing more RAM and a new video card (both can be installed for as little as $150-200).

Do you have children or grandchildren?

If so, don't throw out your ***old*** computer when you upgrade to a newer one.

Clean up your old computer and install:

- a simple word processor
- drawing program (like Broderbund's Kid Pix)
- educational games (there are many good free ones available at download sites on the Web)
- Web browser with filter software

This allows your children to learn, use, and be responsible for a computer without compromising your computer or data if a small hand gets too eager. And if you both need to get a project out, there is no need to rush each other!

Heat danger

If you purchase a computer desk with a built in section for the tower, cut out the backside of it. This will serve two purposes: 1) allows better circulation of air around your computer and 2) easier access to all of the cables attached to the computer.

Also, keep the door open (if it has one) when your computer is running. Again, allowing for better airflow.

Too much heat can cause undo stress and *premature aging* of a computer system.

Should I leave the computer on all the time?

If I had a nickel . . .

I could write volumes about the pros and cons on this one, but here is my best advice.

If you use your computer often throughout the day, then leave it on throughout the day. Turning it off before you go to bed depends on when your bedtime is. If you go to bed at one in the morning and someone's using the computer again at 5:00 a.m., leave it on.

On the other hand, if you turn in around 9-10:00 p.m. and don't use the computer again until nine or later the next morning, go ahead and turn the system off.

If you only use your computer once a day, turn it on when you use it and then shut it off when you finish.

For those in the "mostly on" camp, your computer will run better if you at least restart the system every couple of days.

Bottom line that almost everyone agrees upon: computers should *not* be turned on and off frequently throughout the day.

Also, be aware that you should be using a surge protector on your system. If you live in an area with frequent electrical storms, the only true protection for your system is unplugging it from the wall.

Troubleshooting 101

We all run into problems with our computers. This section will arm you with a few good hints on how to handle these unexpected and sometimes annoying interruptions.

When a problem does arise, approach the problem methodically and calmly. Getting flustered or rushing to find a solution often times exacerbates the problem.

Most valuable tool

If a scanner, printer, modem or piece of software acts sluggish or doesn't respond normally and it was just fine yesterday, shut down and restart your computer.

Restarting your computer can solve ninety percent of little problems that creep up.

Program stops responding

If a program stops reacting to your mouse or keyboard commands follow this procedure:

1. Press CTRL+ALT+DELETE on your keyboard all at the same time to invoke the Close Program dialog box.

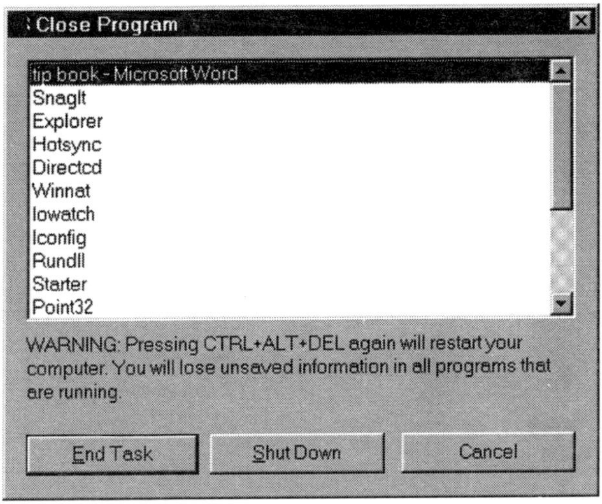

2. Find the program that is not responding (usually the first one).
3. Click one time on it to highlight it.
4. Click on the END TASK button.
5. Wait a few seconds and the program should shut down (you will lose any data that was entered since the last time you saved the file).
6. After it closes, restart the program and all should be well.

NOTE: If the program does not shut down the first time, follow steps 1-5 again.

Blue screen of death

Occasionally, your system may become unstable to the point where you are faced with the dreaded b*lue screen of death*. Really, that's what it's called.

The blue screen of death (BSOD) indicates that our system no longer knows which way is up and needs to be restarted. As with the unresponsive program, any work you have done when this occurs will be lost.

When the BSOD rears its ugly head, push Ctrl+Alt+Delete on your keyboard. If that doesn't work, then simply turn your computer off either at the switch or by disconnecting the power.

If you must shut the system off in this manner, wait about one minute before plugging the machine in or turning it on.

There are many potential causes of the BSOD, but the most common is running out of available memory (temporary RAM).

Preventing data loss

To avoid losing precious computer data from the above two problems, practice good file saving habits:

➲ Name and save your document or computer file to disk before you start working on it.

➲ As you are working on the file/document, make it a habit to save the document at least every ten minutes by either clicking on FILE → SAVE, Ctrl+S from the keyboard, or clicking on the SAVE button from your toolbar.

Computer maintenance

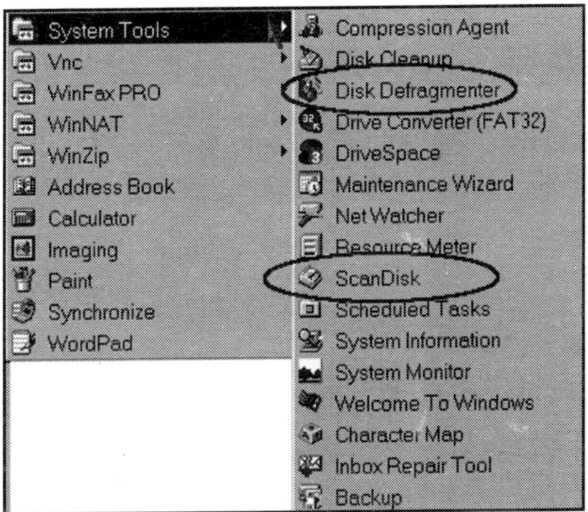

Performing regular maintenance prevents computers from having problems as often. Regular Scan Disk (once every week to ten days) and Defragmenting (once every six to eight weeks) of your computer form the base of a preventative routine. Both can be found by:

1. Click on START.
2. Click on PROGRAMS.
3. Click on ACCESSORIES.
4. Click on SYSTEM TOOLS.

Set your Scan Disk options as pictured on the next page. If you have more than one hard drive, hold down your control key on your keyboard as you click on the drives to select them all.

A thorough Scan Disk only needs to be done a couple of times per year (it takes more than an hour in some cases as compared to less than four minutes with the standard option).

If you use your computer more than just a few hours a week, then you can perform these maintenance activities more frequently.

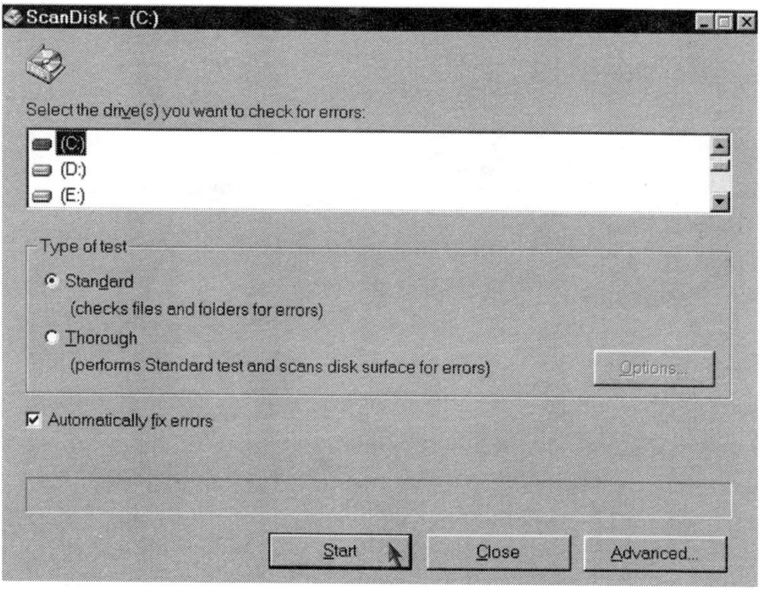

Anti-virus software

Like insurance, anti-virus software protects our computers from the nearly fifty thousand computer viruses competing to cause havoc in our systems.

Many computers come pre-loaded with anti-virus software, but few computer users realize the importance of updating the virus program. The programs work by calling upon an internal database (known as virus definitions) of *known* viruses and how to combat them. If the program's database is not updated regularly, it will not be able fight off the newest viruses.

I recommend the Norton AntiVirus software from Symantec. Norton's update feature remains one of the easiest to perform with or without an Internet connection.

No matter what anti-virus program you use, update it at least once every six weeks. If you use the Norton AntiVirus program, the feat is accomplished via its Live Update program.

Check the help menus of the program you use to learn how to update the definitions.

Keyboard shortcuts

Function	Key Combination
Help	F1
Open Start menu	CTRL+ESC
Switch between open programs	ALT+TAB
Quit program	ALT+F4
Delete items permanently	SHIFT+DELETE
Copy	CTRL+C
Cut	CTRL+X
Paste	CTRL+V
Undo	CTRL+Z
Bold	CTRL+B
Underline	CTRL+U
Switch to another running application.	ALT+TAB
Press down and hold the SHIFT key while you insert a CD-ROM to bypass the auto-run feature.	SHIFT
Close the current window.	ALT+ F4
Opens a drop-down list box.	ALT+DOWN ARROW

Function	**Key Combination**
Switch between multiple windows in the same program.	ALT+F6
Move to the next control in the dialog box.	TAB
Move to the previous control in the dialog box.	SHIFT+TAB
Equivalent to clicking the selected button (the button with the outline)	ENTER
Equivalent to clicking the Cancel button.	ESC

About the author

Rick Castellini's first career was in physical therapy. Like many people, Rick found that the computer could increase his efficiency if used properly. He quickly mastered basic computer skills and learned to use the computer to his advantage.

In 1993, Rick started his computer training and troubleshooting business. His practical experience and straightforward style contribute to its success.

In addition to helping countless individuals and businesses with computer training, Rick has given seminars to many companies including Chevron Oil, the United States Health Care and Finance Administration, United States Geological Survey, and Sun Health Corporation.

Rick shares his expertise weekly on his regional talk radio show, "Castellini on Computers". The show is broadcast in Colorado, Utah, Wyoming and live on the Internet.

Rick is available for keynote speeches, business training seminars, private consulting, workshops and more.

Rick Castellini can be contacted by writing to him via his Web site at:

www.yourpcpartner.com or
email directly to: rick@yourpcpartner.com

INDEX

T

U

V

W

Y

Z